C000051105

ICC CRICKET WORLD CUP
ENGLAND & WALES
2019

THE OFFICIAL BOOK

ICC CRICKET WORLD CUP
ENGLAND & WALES
2019

Published under licence by
Carlton Books Limited,
20 Mortimer Street,
London W1T 3JW

Copyright © Carlton Books Limited 2019

All rights reserved. No part of this publication
may be reproduced, stored in a retrieval system,
or transmitted in any form or by any means,
electronic, mechanical, photocopying, recording
or otherwise, without the permission of the
copyright owner and the publishers.

TM *ICC* Business Corporation FZ LLC 2018. All
rights reserved.

A CIP catalogue record for this book is available
from the British Library.

ISBN 978-1-78739-219-9

Editorial Director: Martin Corteel
Design Manager: Luke Griffin
Designer: Darren Jordan
Picture Research: Paul Langan
Production: Rachel Burgess

Printed in Spain

ICC CRICKET WORLD CUP

ENGLAND & WALES

2019

THE OFFICIAL BOOK

Chris Hawkes

CONTENTS

Opposite: *With fireworks exploding overhead Australia's players run onto the field after their team had won the ICC Cricket World Cup 2015 final.*

Next pages: *Australia's players celebrate after becoming world champions in 2015, but which team will take home the trophy on 14 July?*

Below: *The famous Father Time weather vane at Lord's. No one knows if Father Time is placing the bails on the stumps to start play or removing them at the end of the day.*

INTRODUCTION

Welcome to the *ICC* Cricket World Cup 2019 Official Book. The 12th edition of one-day international cricket's most-eagerly anticipated showpiece event will take place in England and Wales between May and July 2019 and will be staged at 11 grounds, from Chester-le-Street in the north of England to Southampton on the south coast and taking in the Welsh capital Cardiff en route. The final, naturally, will be staged at the game's most iconic venue, Lord's Cricket Ground in St John's Wood, London. Ten teams will vie for the honour of being crowned as the game's world champions.

THE *ICC* CRICKET WORLD CUP has a rich history, and has grown beyond all recognition. When eight teams arrived in England back in 1975 to contest the first edition of the tournament, no one quite knew what to expect, including the players. This time, the competitors will gather in England and Wales knowing that the world's eyes will be upon them. Such has been the amazing progress of the tournament, it is now the third most-watched sporting event in the world, behind only the FIFA World Cup and the Olympic Games.

This book covers every angle of the tournament. There is a report on each of the previous editions of the event. Every team is looked at in detail, including Afghanistan, whose rise to the top table of international cricket has produced one of the most uplifting stories in world sport over recent years, and then we take a look at a gallery of players whose names could well dominate the headlines during the tournament itself.

As ever, compiling such a book has been the work of many people. As is the case for all who write on cricket, our task is made so much easier by the many statisticians around the world who have recorded every game in detail over the years. I would also like to thank Martin Corteel for his endless encouragement and patience while putting this book together; Luke Griffin for his design skill in bringing each of the pages to life; and Paul Langan for the hours he has spent rooting through the photo archives to discover some of the game's most iconic images.

Enjoy the book and enjoy the tournament!

WELCOME TO ENGLAND & WALES

The 12th edition of the *ICC* Cricket World Cup will be staged in England and Wales for the first time since 1999. It will be the fifth time England has hosted the event, and the second time that matches in the tournament will take place in Wales. It is a worthy venue: this is the island to which cricket can trace its origins and it has a rich cricket history that stretches back over 400 years.

Opposite: *The Oval is certain to be packed on 30 May 2019, when England meet South Africa in the opening match of the ICC Cricket World Cup.*

SETTING THE SCENE FOR CWC19

It is hard to explain to those new to the tournament just how much the *ICC* Cricket World Cup has grown since it was first contested back in 1975. Back then, the one-day game was still very much in its infancy (only 18 one-day internationals had ever been played by the time the players arrived in England) and few, if any, knew what to expect – including the players. And nobody knew what to call it either.

Opposite: Pakistan's jublilant captain Sarfraz Ahmed shows off the ICC Champions Trophy 2017 after the 180-run defeat of India in the final at The Oval.

Below: Spectators watch a giant screen in Victoria Square at the Birmingham Fan Zone during the ICC Champions Trophy 2017.

THE *ICC* WERE RELUCTANT to call it the World Cup, fearing that to give it such a grand title would diminish the status of Test cricket – still, to this day, the game's dominant and most-revered format. It was the British press who settled that argument: rather than referring to it as the "International Tournament", the papers settled on the term "World Cup" and the title stuck. Despite the uncertainty, the tournament was a success. As the great West Indian commentator Tony Cozier reflected at the time, it was "perhaps the boldest and most ambitious innovation the game has known since the legalization of overarm bowling". And, crucially, the public embraced it, too: that year, aggregate crowds of 158,000 (an average of just over 10,500 spectators per match) paid over £200,000 (a considerable sum of money at the time) to watch the tournament's 15 matches.

Fast-forward 40 years and by 2015 the *ICC* Cricket World Cup had become the third most-watched sporting event in the world, after the Football World Cup and the Olympic Games. The *ICC* Cricket World Cup 2015, held in Australia and New Zealand, attracted an estimated television audience of 1.5 billion viewers in 220 territories around the world and generated AU$1 billion (just over £500 million) in direct spending. The final itself, contested by the co-hosts, drew a crowd of 93,013 spectators to the Melbourne Cricket Ground – a record for an *ICC* Cricket

World Cup final. These are staggering numbers by any measure.

If all the above goes to show just how firmly established the *ICC* Cricket World Cup has become as a global sporting event, it also suggests that the 2019 edition of the event has an awful lot to live up to. It could not, perhaps, have chosen a better venue than England and Wales as a platform upon which to continue its expansion.

The game can trace its roots to these shores and it remains cricket's spiritual home. It also has one of the most diverse fan-bases in world cricket. Britain's culturally diverse population means that every one of the ten teams participating at the event can expect to be generously supported, as for many British-born fans their cricketing loyalties often lie in the land of their grandparents, be it from Asia or the Caribbean. This has been shown to great effect by two recent *ICC* events that have been staged here: the *ICC* Champions Trophy 2017 and the *ICC* Women's World Cup 2017.

The 2017 *ICC* Champions Trophy, featuring the world's eight top-ranked one-day international countries, generated enormous interest and drew in spectators in huge numbers. The final itself, between India and Pakistan, had a rumoured (albeit not confirmed) one billion people worldwide tune in to watch it. Around 26,000 flag-waving fans descended on The Oval to view the spectacle but, for those watching the match on television, you could have been forgiven for thinking that the game was taking place in either Mumbai or Lahore rather than in the backstreets of Kennington, London.

There was tremendous enthusiasm for the 2017 *ICC* Women's World Cup, too. It broke all previous records for the tournament. The global television audience increased by 80 per cent from the previous edition of the competition in 2013, with more than 50 million viewers tuning in worldwide. And the final itself, contested between hosts England and India at Lord's, was played before a sell-out crowd of 26,500 – the highest attendance ever at an *ICC* Women's World Cup match.

You can expect more of the same at the *ICC* Cricket World Cup 2019. All 48 matches, played at 11 world-class venues across England and Wales, will be sold out. Fans will be there in force both inside the ground and at various viewing zones dotted around the United Kingdom. The timing of the tournament, in the early British summer, should provide for some hugely entertaining cricket, too. The pitches should help the bowlers, thus creating even contests between bat and ball. There is every indication that the *ICC* Cricket World Cup 2019 will be the best yet.

TOURNAMENT STRUCTURE & RULES

There has been much debate over the years as to how best to structure the *ICC* Cricket World Cup. What tournament format works best? How do you give lower-ranked teams a fair chance of achieving at least one victory at the tournament or at least providing them with a means of taking positives from the competition?

HOW DO YOU MAINTAIN PROLONGED spectator interest in the event? How can you avoid an endless list of dead-rubber matches in which teams have nothing left to play for? How can you ensure that spectators, many of whom have travelled from the other side of the globe, get to see their team perform as much as possible?

For many, the best structure at an *ICC* Cricket World Cup in recent years came at the 1992 tournament staged in Australia and New Zealand. There, the group stage consisted, quite simply, of every team in the tournament playing the other, with the top-four teams at the end of the group-stage round of matches proceeding to the semi-finals. And it is to that format which the *ICC* Cricket World Cup 2019 will return – albeit with ten teams, as opposed to nine, on this occasion. This means that a total of 48 matches will be played, and there will be a guarantee of some mouth-watering clashes over the course of the tournament's 46 days: India against Pakistan at Old Trafford on 16 June and England against Australia at Lord's on 25 June to name but two.

There are practical reasons for returning to this much-celebrated format. It is more player-friendly: it allows for teams to have greater recovery time between matches – some teams will have up to five days between matches. It caters for the fans, too: it gives them at least nine chances to catch a glimpse of their favourite team and they will know exactly where their team will be for several weeks, rather than

having to plot a course through the knockout brackets – if my team finishes first or second in a group they will play either here, or there. It also, most significantly perhaps, gives the tournament an opportunity to tap into the UK's multi-cultural population, in which the loyalties of British-born cricket fans could lie with a number of different participants. As the tournament's managing director Steve Elworthy, who represented South Africa at the *ICC* Cricket World Cup 1999, said: "Because of the UK's diverse population, every team will be guaranteed a 'home crowd' every time they play at some of the most iconic grounds in the world."

Opposite: Pakistan's fans had plenty to cheer about in the ICC Champions Trophy 2017 final at The Oval.

TOURNAMENT RULES

Key rules for the *ICC* Cricket World Cup 2019:

Points

Win – 2 points

Tie/No result/Match abandoned – 1 point

Loss – 0 points

Tie – when all the innings have been completed and the scores are equal (no account shall be taken of the number of wickets that have fallen).

No result – declared if neither side has had the opportunity of batting for 10 overs.

In the event of teams finishing on equal points in the group, the ordering of teams will be decided in the following order of priority:

(i) The team with the most wins in the group matches will be placed in the higher position.

(ii) If there are teams with equal points and equal wins in the group matches, then in such circumstances the team with the higher net run-rate in the group matches will be placed in the higher position;

(iii) If two or more teams are still equal, they will be ordered according to the head-to-head match played between them (points then net run-rate in those matches).

In the event of a tied semi-final or final, the teams shall compete in a Super Over to determine which side is the winner.

POWER PLAYS

Each innings will consist of three power plays.

Power play 1: no more than two fielders shall be permitted outside the fielding restriction area for overs 1 to 10 inclusive.

Power play 2: no more than four fielders shall be permitted outside the fielding restriction area for overs 11 to 40 inclusive.

Power play 3: no more than five fielders shall be permitted outside the fielding restriction area for overs 41 to 50 inclusive.

Rain rule: revised targets in the event of rain interruptions shall be calculated using the Duckworth/Lewis/Stern method.

ENGLISH CRICKET HERITAGE

As is the case with most sports, the actual origins of cricket are uncertain. Some claim the game was created in France, some say it can be traced to Flanders, Belgium, while others suggest that the game was first played in southern England. What is certain, is that the game first took root in England on a widespread basis and that, from there, it was introduced to every corner of the world via both the British Empire and Britain's extensive global trade connections.

Below: With a career that spanned 35 years, W.G. Grace was a leading light of cricket's Victorian era.

Opposite: Pakistan's Javed Miandad hits out against England during the 1992 ICC Cricket World Cup – the first in which teams played in coloured clothing.

Village green origins

The first reference to the game came during a court case in Guildford, Surrey, in 1598, in which 59-year-old John Derrick testified that he and his friends had played a game he called "creckett" some 50 years earlier. This confirmed that a form of cricket had been played by children since at least the 1540s. The first accepted reference to the game being played by adults came in 1611, when two men in Sussex were prosecuted for playing cricket instead of attending church on a Sunday. Village cricket became commonplace in southern England by the end of the 17th century.

W.G. Grace and the Victorians

Even though an unofficial version of the competition had been contested since 1864, an official County Championship finally got off the ground in 1890, with Surrey winning five of the first six titles. This was the so-called Golden Age of Cricket, a period that continues to evoke great nostalgia and a feeling that the game has never been played in greater spirit or with a greater sense of fairness since. What is certainly true is that this period spawned some of English cricket's greatest-ever names: W.G. Grace, Wilfred Rhodes, C.B. Fry, Ranjitsinhji and Victor Trumper to name but a few.

Bodyline series

Donald Bradman's prolific run-scoring during the 1930 Ashes series, which included an imperious 334 at Headingley, led England to deploy some hugely controversial tactics when they travelled to Australia in 1932–33. In an attempt to subdue Bradman, England's captain, Douglas Jardine, devised his fast-leg bowling theory, instructing his fast bowlers to aim for the batsman's body with short, fast, hostile bowling. The tactic – now immortalized by the word "Bodyline" – may have won Jardine the Ashes 4–1, but it gained England few friends. The subsequent outcry led to huge diplomatic tension between the two countries.

One-day cricket

When one-day international cricket first arrived on the international cricket scene in the early 1970s, the format provided cricket's authorities with the means of hosting a tournament to decide a world champion – a *ICC* Cricket World Cup. When the idea of staging such a tournament was first mooted, there was only one contender to host the event. England had the resources to stage the event and it made absolute sense to crown the game's first world champions in the country where it had all begun. The tournament was staged in 1975, with the Windies crowned the game's first champions at Lord's.

Post-WW2 rebirth

The Second World War had stopped cricket in its tracks, as many of England's players swapped their whites for full battle gear, but the late 1940s and early 1950s saw the emergence of some of the giants of the English game. Len Hutton and Denis Compton established themselves as players of effortless class, while, with the ball, fast bowler Frank "Typhoon" Tyson struck fear into the hearts of batsmen around the world and Jim Laker continued England's tradition of producing high quality spin bowlers, as evidenced by his world-record match haul of 19 for 90 against Australia at Old Trafford in 1956.

Pyjama cricket

Players wearing coloured clothing – known in its early days in the 1970s as "pyjama cricket" – is a relatively recent development in the long history of the game. Originating in Australia during the 1970s, the practice proved popular given the increasing number of viewers watching cricket in colour on television, and it quickly caught on in the various non-Test forms of the game. English cricket held out for a number of years, until it finally embraced coloured clothing in 1993, when counties wore coloured outfits in that year's Sunday League 40-over competition. They have remained a staple ever since.

CRICKET WORLD CUP FAST SHOW

A match at the 2019 *ICC* Cricket World Cup provides the perfect day out for the entire family and a memorable meeting point for friends. But what is different about one-day cricket, and what should fans who are new to the game be looking out for? Here are a few pointers.

Day-night cricket

Although the first cricket match under floodlights was played in August 1952 (a benefit match for former England player Jack Young between Middlesex CCC and Arsenal FC at Highbury Stadium, London), day-night cricket – a game that starts in the afternoon and ends at night under floodlights – achieved popularity for the first time in the late 1970s during World Series Cricket. The first one-day international under lights was played in November 1979, between Australia and the Windies, and day-night matches have been a permanent feature of the game, both at domestic and international level, ever since.

Third-umpire adjudications

The third umpire is an umpire who, when asked by the on-field umpires or the players, reviews certain decisions, such as lbws, run-outs, stumpings, debated catches and no-balls. They have been an accepted, and universally embraced, part of the game since November 1992, when they featured for the first time in a Test match between South Africa and India in Durban. Today, each team can ask for the on-field umpire's decision to be checked, but the number of reviews is limited. Since this system came in force in 2009, one in four reviews have resulted in the original decision being overturned.

Power hitting

How the game of cricket has changed. There was a time when a beautifully timed, crisp cover drive was deemed to be the pinnacle of batting. Nowadays, the art of batsmanship is all about big hitting. Why settle for four runs when the same simple swipe of a bat can bring you six? Power hitting is all about bigger, heavier bats, increased bat speed and the greater physical strength of batsmen. And who is the modern game's most consistent big hitter? India's Rohit Sharma holds the record for the most sixes hit in international cricket in a calendar year, with 69 in 2017.

Death bowling

The art of bowling in the final overs of an innings – commonly known as "death bowling" – is a prized commodity in cricket, and those bowlers who can consistently produce the goods and dry up an opponent's flow of runs at that time are prized assets in any team. So what makes for the perfect death bowler? There are many attributes including: (i) having the right plans in place for each of the batsmen; (ii) being able to bowl the perfect yorker at the perfect time; and (iii) being able to hold your nerve when the pressure is well and truly on.

Fancy-dress fans

Cricket has become the day out of choice for many, be it a family, a group of work colleagues or those on a stag- or hen-do. And some have taken the fun to extraordinary levels: cast your eyes around the average crowd at a one-day international and you'll see a collection of fancy-dress outfits. There's often a Cookie Monster, a group of men dressed up in full kit ready to go out and bat, a variety of Super Marios, a variety of nuns and, more often than not, one corner of the ground is home to a group of Ritchie Benauds.

Opposite: *The Sydney Cricket Ground looking resplendent under lights. Day-night cricket really took off in Australia in the 1970s during World Series Cricket.*

Right: *Adding colour and noise, England's "Barmy Army" help to create a vibrant atmosphere where ever they go.*

The Barmy Army

England's cricket fans are among the most loyal and passionate in the world. Few countries can boast as much support as England when they travel overseas. Recent England overseas tours have attracted a huge following and they now have their own name, the "Barmy Army". Famed for their witty songs, chants and undying support, many of cricket's biggest names have been on the receiving end of their mirth. Some never flinched (such as Shane Warne), but others fared less well, and their performances dipped noticeably in the face of the comments aimed towards them.

THE VENUES

The *ICC* Cricket World Cup 2019 will comprise of 48 matches over the course of 46 days. The tournament will travel the length and breadth of England, with four matches also taking place in Wales, at Sophia Gardens in Cardiff.

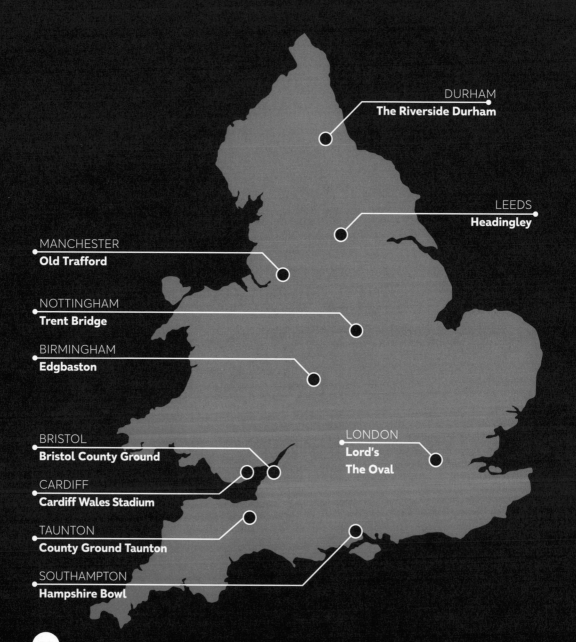

DURHAM
The Riverside Durham

LEEDS
Headingley

MANCHESTER
Old Trafford

NOTTINGHAM
Trent Bridge

BIRMINGHAM
Edgbaston

BRISTOL
Bristol County Ground

LONDON
Lord's
The Oval

CARDIFF
Cardiff Wales Stadium

TAUNTON
County Ground Taunton

SOUTHAMPTON
Hampshire Bowl

HAMPSHIRE BOWL

Designed by award-winning architects Michael Hopkins & Partners, the state-of-the-art Hampshire Bowl, on the outskirts of Southampton, was completed in 2001, hosted its first international match two years later (a one-day international between South Africa and Zimbabwe) and, in 2011, became England's tenth Test venue when England hosted Sri Lanka. It will host five matches during the *ICC* Cricket World Cup 2019.

Location: Southampton
Capacity: 17,000
CWC 2019 matches:
5 June 2019 (10:30) –
        India v South Africa
10 June 2019 (10:30) –
        South Africa v West Indies
14 June 2019 (10:30) –
        England v West Indies
22 June 2019 (10:30) –
        Afghanistan v India
24 June 2019 (10:30) –
        Afghanistan v Bangladesh

BRISTOL COUNTY GROUND

Established in 1889, when it was bought by W.G. Grace, the Bristol County Ground in Bristol (home to Gloucestershire CCC) is full of character. It is steeped in rich cricket history, too, for this was the ground at which the likes of Grace, Gilbert Jessop and Wally Hammond plied their trade in county cricket. It hosted its first one-day international at the 1983 *ICC* Cricket World Cup (New Zealand v Sri Lanka) and three matches will be played here during the 2019 tournament.

Location: Bristol
Capacity: 11,000
CWC 2019 matches:
1 June 2019 (13:30 – D/N) –
        Australia v Afghanistan
7 June 2019 (10:30) –
        Pakistan v Sri Lanka
11 June 2019 (10:30) –
        Bangladesh v Sri Lanka

COUNTY GROUND TAUNTON

Located in the centre of Taunton, the County Ground Taunton is the most south-westerly of England's county grounds. Established in 1882, it was the place to be during the 1980s when Ian Botham, Viv Richards and Joel Garner propelled Somerset to the top of the county game. It hosted its first one-day international during the *ICC* Cricket World Cup 1983, has been the official home of the England Women's team since 2006 and will host three matches during the 2019 tournament.

Location: Taunton
Capacity: 8,000
CWC 2019 matches:
8 June 2019 (13:30 – D/N) –
        Afghanistan v New Zealand
12 June 2019 (10:30) –
        Australia v Pakistan
17 June 2019 (10:30) –
        Bangladesh v West Indies

CARDIFF WALES STADIUM

The only venue at the *ICC* Cricket World Cup 2019 in Wales, Cardiff Wales Stadium has been the official home of Glamorgan since 1995, prior to which the county led a particularly nomadic existence. The ground underwent a major redevelopment in the late 1990s, becoming a regular one-day international venue ever since and hosted its first Test match during the 2009 Ashes series. Four matches will be played here during the 2019 tournament, including the day-night match between Afghanistan and South Africa.

Location: Cardiff
Capacity: 15,200
CWC 2019 matches:
1 June 2019 (10:30) –
        New Zealand v Sri Lanka
4 June 2019 (10:30) –
        Afghanistan v Sri Lanka
8 June 2019 (10:30) –
        England v Bangladesh
15 June 2019 (13:30 – D/N) –
        Afghanistan v South Africa

EDGBASTON

Established in 1882 in a leafy suburb of Birmingham, Edgbaston hosted only four matches in its first 27 years, but has become one of the most revered Test-match venues in world cricket. The scene of Brian Lara's first-class world-record 501 not out in 1994, it has been the scene for several standout moments in cricket's history, including Ian Botham's 5 for 11 during the 1981 Ashes series and England memorable 2-run victory over Australia in 2005. It will host five matches during the *ICC* Cricket World Cup 2019, including the second semi-final.

Location: Birmingham
Capacity: 24,500
CWC 2019 matches:
19 June 2019 (10:30) –
      New Zealand v South Africa
26 June 2019 (10:30) –
      New Zealand v Pakistan
30 June 2019 (10:30) –
      England v India
2 July 2019 (10:30) –
      Bangladesh v India
11 July 2019 (10:30) – **SEMI-FINAL 2**

THE RIVERSIDE DURHAM

Built in the shadow of Lumley Castle and completed in 1995, the Riverside Durham is the home of England's newest county cricket team, Durham. The ground first staged an international match at the *ICC* Cricket World Cup 1999 (Pakistan v Scotland) and hosted its first Test match later that year when England played Zimbabwe. Now an established international cricket venue, it will host three matches at the *ICC* Cricket World Cup 2019, including England's clash against New Zealand.

Location: Durham
Capacity: 14,000
CWC 2019 matches:
28 June 2019 (10:30) –
      South Africa v Sri Lanka
1 July 2019 (10:30) –
      Sri Lanka v West Indies
3 July 2019 (10:30) –
      England v New Zealand

HEADINGLEY

Established in 1890, Headingley, the home of Yorkshire CCC, will forever be linked with England's dramatic, come-from-behind, Ian Botham and Bob Willis-inspired, 18-run victory over Australia during the 1981 Ashes. But the ground has also provided the stage for some other remarkable feats, including Don Bradman's two Ashes triple-centuries in 1930 and 1934 and Geoffrey Boycott's 100th first-class 100. It will host four matches during the *ICC* Cricket World Cup 2019, including England's match against Sri Lanka.

Location: Leeds
Capacity: 18,350
CWC 2019 matches:
21 June 2019 (10:30) –
      England v Sri Lanka
29 June 2019 (10:30) –
      Afghanistan v Pakistan
4 July 2019 (10:30) –
      Afghanistan v West Indies
6 July 2019 (10:30) –
      India v Sri Lanka

OLD TRAFFORD

Perhaps one of the most famous corners in English sport, the Old Trafford area is home to both Manchester United and Lancashire CCC. The cricket ground, which stands a few streets away from football's Theatre of Dreams, hosted its first Test match way back in 1884 and etched itself into cricket legend when it provided the stage for the greatest-ever bowling performance in Test cricket: Jim Laker's 19 for 90 against Australia in 1956. It is also going to be staging some potentially compelling matches at the *ICC* Cricket World Cup 2019, including India v Pakistan and the first semi-final.

Location: Manchester
Capacity: 23,000
CWC 2019 matches:
16 June 2019 (10:30) –
      India v Pakistan
18 June 2019 (10:30) –
      England v Afghanistan
22 June 2019 (13:30 – D/N) –
      New Zealand v West Indies
27 June 2019 (10:30) –
      India v West Indies
6 July 2019 (13:30 – D/N) –
      Australia v South Africa
9 July 2019 (10:30) – **SEMI-FINAL 1**

TRENT BRIDGE

An established and popular venue, Trent Bridge has been hosting Test cricket since 1899 and one-day internationals since 1974 (when Pakistan beat England there by seven wickets). It is home to Nottinghamshire CCC and some of the game's greatest names plied their trade in county cricket there, including Harold Larwood, Bill Voce, Gary Sobers, Clive Rice and Richard Hadlee. It will stage five games at the *ICC Cricket World Cup 2019*.

Location: Nottingham
Capacity: 17,000
CWC 2019 matches:
31 May 2019 (10:30) –
    Pakistan v West Indies
3 June 2019 (10:30) –
    England v Pakistan
6 June 2019 (10:30) –
    Australia v West Indies
13 June 2019 (10:30) –
    India v New Zealand
20 June 2019 (10:30) –
    Australia v Bangladesh

THE OVAL

Established in 1845, this is England's oldest ground and the site of England's first-ever Test match on home soil – against Australia in 1880. Set in the heart of London, the ground's character is etched into the minds of every English cricket fan: the imposing pavilion, the gasometers on the east side of the ground and the wicket – considered by many to be the best batting track in England. It will host five matches during the *ICC Cricket World Cup 2019*, including the heavyweight clashes of England v South Africa and Australia v India.

Location: London
Capacity: 25,000
CWC 2019 matches:
30 May 2019 (10:30) –
    England v South Africa
2 June 2019 (10:30) –
    Bangladesh v South Africa
5 June 2019 (13:30 – D/N) –
    Bangladesh v New Zealand
9 June 2019 (10:30) –
    Australia v India
15 June 2019 (10:30) –
    Australia v Sri Lanka

LORD'S

Although it has changed dramatically over the years, this is the one ground that every player in the world dreams of playing at: its fabled pavilion, the ground's endearing slope … everything about it that makes it the spiritual home of cricket. Actually the third ground built by Thomas Lord, Test cricket was first played at Lord's in 1884. It staged its first one-day international in 1972 and four *ICC Cricket World Cup* finals (in 1975, 1979, 1983 and 1999) – more than any other ground in world cricket. It is set to host a fifth in 2019 along with four of the group matches, including England v Australia.

Location: London
Capacity: 28,500
CWC 2019 matches:
23 June 2019 (10:30) –
    Pakistan v South Africa
25 June 2019 (10:30) –
    England v Australia
29 June 2019 (13:30 – D/N) –
    Australia v New Zealand
5 July 2019 (10:30) –
    Bangladesh v Pakistan
14 July 2019 (10:30) –
    CRICKET WORLD CUP FINAL

1 MAGIC MOMENTS:

Viv Richards' final heroics

England were totally on top when Viv Richards strode to the crease in the final of *ICC* Cricket World Cup 1979. Having won the toss and elected to field, they had reduced the Windies to 99 for 4. But the Antiguan produced one of the most memorable knocks in World Cup history: he hammered 138 not out off 157 balls (with 11 fours and three sixes) to guide his side to a competitive total of 286 for 9. It proved too much for England. Openers Mike Brearley and Geoffrey Boycott got them off to a steady start, with a partnership of 129, but it had taken them 38 overs to get there. With the required run-rate soaring, England collapsed dramatically, losing their final eight wickets for 11 runs as the Windies romped to a 92-run victory. The men from the Caribbean, champions four years earlier, had defended their crown, and Viv Richards had been their hero.

Right: Richards' sensational performance in the ICC Cricket World Cup 1979 final came four years after he had helped the Windies win the inaugural tournament in 1975.

THE ROAD TO ENGLAND & WALES

Qualifying events for the *ICC* Cricket World Cup 2019 started back in 2013 with 43 nations vying for a place in the second round of qualifying. Since then, teams from around the world have battled in venues as diverse as Jersey, the United States, Namibia and Uganda. By March 2018, the number of teams had been whittled down to ten: the top-eight ranked teams in the *ICC*'s One-Day International rankings, plus the two qualifiers – the Windies and Afghanistan.

Opposite: *Afghanistan went from the brink of elimination from Group B to winning the ICC Cricket World Cup 2019 qualifying tournament by winning their last five matches, including the final against fellow qualifiers Windies in Harare, Zimbabwe, in March 2018.*

HOW THE TEAMS QUALIFIED

The journey to the *ICC* Cricket World Cup 2019 started way back in 2013, with a series of events, contested across five regions: Africa, the Americas, Asia, East Asia-Pacific and Europe. These events, in which 43 nations took part, had a divisional structure, with promotion and relegation.

Below: Afghanistan's troubled past was forgotten in March 2018 as they celebrated victory in the ICC Cricket World Cup 2019 qualifying tournament.

THE PROMOTED TEAMS from each regional division then progressed to a global qualification process in which sides were whittled down through a series of league-based tournaments.

This started with the *ICC* World Cricket League Division Six, played in England in September 2015, which saw Guernsey and Vanuatu promoted to Division Five. *ICC* WCL Division Five matches took place in Jersey in May 2016, with Oman and Jersey promoted to Division Four. Matches in the *ICC* WCL Division Four took place in the United States in October–November 2016, and resulted in Oman and the United States being promoted to Division Three. The *ICC* WCL Division Three tournament, staged in Uganda in May 2017, saw Oman and Canada gain promotion to Division Two And then the qualification process started to get serious – at last, the teams still standing

could sniff a shot at qualification for the tournament proper. The Division Two tournament, in which the top-two teams gained a place in the main *ICC Cricket World Cup qualifying* tournament (staged in Zimbabwe in March 2018), took place in Namibia in February 2018: Nepal and the United Arab Emirates took the spoils.

While the above had been going on, the best of the rest in cricketing terms, had been playing in the highest tier of cricket played by non-Test-playing nations: the *ICC* World Cricket League Championship. This consisted of each of the eight teams in the league playing the other twice between June 2015 and December 2017, with the top four teams progressing to the *ICC* Cricket World Cup qualifying tournament in Zimbabwe. By the time the 56 matches had been completed, the Netherlands, Scotland, Hong Kong and Papua New Guinea stood in the top-four places. We now had six teams qualified for Zimbabwe: the above four, plus Oman and the United Arab Emirates. These would be joined in Zimbabwe by the Windies, Afghanistan, Ireland and Zimbabwe – and the stakes could not have been higher: ten teams fighting it out for the two available qualification spots for the *ICC* Cricket World Cup 2019.

The qualifying tournament in Zimbabwe in March 2018 was full of intrigue and drama. The ten teams were split into two groups of five, in which each team would play the other, with the top three teams in the group progressing to a Super Six stage – the top-two teams following the Super Sixes would qualify for the *ICC* Cricket World Cup 2019 and would contest a final.

In Group A, the United Arab Emirates opened their tournament account with a comfortable 56-run victory over Papua New Guinea. Elsewhere, Ireland got their campaign off to a cracking start with a thumping 93-run victory over the Netherlands. The Irish made it two wins from two when they beat Papua New Guinea by four wickets in their second match. Tony Ura hit an eye-catching 142-ball 151 as Papua New Guinea posted 235 all out, but Ireland captain William Porterfield responded with a century of his own (111) to see his side home with four wickets in hand and with five balls to spare.

Two-time *ICC* Cricket World Cup champions Windies started their tournament in eye-catching style against the United Arab Emirates. Shimron Hetmyer smashed a 93-ball 127 as the Windies posted an impressive 357 for 4, while Jason Holder took 5 for 53 as the United Arab Emirates could only muster 297 for 6 in reply. In the third round of matches, the United Arab Emirates posted their second victory of the campaign with a six-wicket victory over the Netherlands (with off-spinner Rohan Mustafa taking 5 for 26), while the Windies continued their winning ways with a comfortable six-wicket victory over Papua New Guinea, in which Carlos Braithwaite (5 for 27) shone with the ball and Jason Holder (99 not out) led from the front with the bat.

The fourth round of matches in Group A saw a clash of the tournament's big guns, when the Windies played Ireland. The Windies, put into bat, slipped to 83 for 5 in the 19th over before Rovman Powell saved the day, hitting 101 to lead his side's recovery to 257 for 8. It proved too much for Ireland: Ed Joyce hit a patient 86-ball 63 but, although he received support from Niall O'Brien (34) and his brother Kevin O'Brien (38), Ireland slipped to 205 all out and to defeat by 52 runs. Victory secured the Windies' place in the Super Sixes. Elsewhere, the Netherlands beat Papua New Guinea by 57 runs. The Windies rounded out their group campaign with a 54-run victory over the Netherlands, while Ireland thumped the already qualified United Arab Emirates by 226 runs to secure the group's final berth in the Super Sixes.

Group B – featuring Afghanistan, Hong Kong, Nepal, Scotland and Zimbabwe – was full of drama and the fight for the three Super Six qualifying spots went down to the final round of matches. In the opening round of games, Zimbabwe beat Nepal by 116 runs, while Scotland proved too strong for Afghanistan, winning by seven wickets. Scotland continued their winning ways with a nervy four-wicket win over Hong Kong, losing six wickets chasing just 92 for victory, while Zimbabwe edged past Afghanistan in a thriller. Batting first, Zimbabwe had slipped to 196 all out, with Rashid Khan taking 3 for 38, but Afghanistan's chase fell agonizingly short: they fell to 194 all out in the final over of the match. In the third round of matches, Scotland beat Nepal by four wickets to secure their place in the Super Sixes, while *ICC* Cricket World

Below: *Jason Holder scored 99 not out in the Windies' six-wicket victory over Papua New Guinea in the ICC Cricket World Cup qualifying tournament.*

Cup 2015 participant Afghanistan slipped to defeat by 30 runs to Hong Kong to leave their hopes hanging by a thread. It was Afghanistan's third defeat in as many games; for Hong Kong, however, it was a first-ever one-day international victory against a full member side. In the fourth round of matches, Zimbabwe beat Hong Kong by 89 runs to secure their place in the Super Sixes, while, finally, Afghanistan posted their first victory of the tournament – by six wickets against Nepal – to keep their faint hopes of progressing alive. They needed a helping hand from Nepal to do so, however. If Hong Kong beat Nepal in the final round of matches, they would qualify at Afghanistan's expense. But they lost – by five wickets. Zimbabwe and Scotland, already through to the Super Sixes, tied the group's final match.

In the Super Sixes, teams would keep any points they had gained against fellow qualifiers from their group and play further matches against the teams that had qualified from the other group. That meant that Afghanistan started the Super Sixes with no points and, realistically, had

ICC Cricket World Cup QUALIFYING TOURNAMENT

Leading run-scorers: top five

Pos	Runs	Player (country)
1	357	Brendan Taylor (Zimbabwe)
2	288	Calum MacLeod (Scotland)
3	267	Peter Stirling (Ireland)
4	257	Mohammad Nabi (Afghanistan)
5	247	William Porterfield (Ireland)

Leading wicket-takers: top five

Pos	Wickets	Player (country)
1	16	Mujeeb Ur Rahman (Afghanistan)
2	15	Safyaan Sharif (Scotland)
=	15	Jason Holder (Windies)
4	14	Rashid Khan (Afghanistan)
5	13	Boyd Rankin (Ireland)
=	13	Mohammad Naveed (United Arab Emirates)

to win all three of their matches if they were to qualify for the *ICC* Cricket World Cup 2019. Their first opponent in the Super Sixes: the Windies. Afghanistan were magnificent: they restricted the Windies to 197 for 8 and held their nerve with the bat to win by three wickets. Elsewhere, Scotland beat the United Arab Emirates by 73 runs; Zimbabwe cruised to a 107-run victory over Ireland; Ireland got their hopes back on track with a 25-run victory over Scotland; and the Windies beat Zimbabwe by four wickets. The upshot of all of this was that no side could exert its dominance over the others; all of which gave Afghanistan a chance. And those chances increased when Afghanistan beat the United Arab Emirates by five wickets. The Windies beat Scotland by five runs to secure the first of the qualification berths for the *ICC* Cricket World Cup 2019, while Zimbabwe's hopes of securing the other ended when they slumped to a surprise three-run defeat to the United Arab Emirates. All of which meant that the final match of the Super Sixes – Ireland against Afghanistan – came

down to a winner-takes-all affair. Ireland batted first and struggled to 209 for 7; Afghanistan completed their remarkable turnaround by reaching the target for the loss of five wickets with five balls to spare. And, just to show it had not been a fluke, went on to beat the Windies by seven wickets in the final, too.

A remarkable qualifying process, that had lasted almost five years, had produced its two qualifiers: the Windies and Afghanistan. While qualification might have been expected for the Windies, Afghanistan's remarkable turnaround in form was one of world cricket's greatest escapes. "We didn't even have a 10 per cent chance to qualify after the first round," said captain Asghar Stanikzai, "but after some support from people back home, the prayers of the people of Afghanistan, all the messages we received, all the messages on social media, it was not just the dream for our guys, but it was the dream of all Afghanistan as well. I can't express how important it was for us, and for Afghanistan, to qualify for the 2019 World Cup."

JOURNEY TO THE
ICC Cricket World Cup 2019

ICC CRICKET WORLD CUP QUALIFIERS
Zimbabwe, March 2018: Qualifiers; Afghanistan and the Windies

ICC WORLD CRICKET LEAGUE
June 2015–December 2017
Qualifiers:
Netherlands
Scotland
Hong Kong
Papua New Guinea

ICC WORLD CRICKET LEAGUE DIVISION TWO
Namibia, February 2019
Qualifiers: Nepal and United Arab Emirates

ICC WORLD CRICKET LEAGUE DIVISION THREE
Uganda, 23–30 May 2017
Promoted: Oman and Canada

ICC WORLD CRICKET LEAGUE DIVISION FOUR
USA, 29 October–5 November 2016
Promoted: Oman and USA

ICC WORLD CRICKET LEAGUE DIVISION FIVE
Jersey; 21–28 May 2016
Promoted: Oman and Jersey

ICC WORLD CRICKET LEAGUE DIVISION SIX
England, 7–13 September 2015
Promoted: Guernsey and Vanuata

REGIONAL QUALIFIERS

MRF TYRES
ICC WORLD CRICKET RANKINGS

Team Rankings (as of 13 February 2019)

1 England
2 India
3 New Zealand
4 South Africa
5 Pakistan
6 Australia
7 Bangladesh
8 Sri Lanka
9 Windies
10 Afghanistan

Opposite: India may rank behind England in the ICC World Cricket rankings, but in Jasprit Bumrah they have the world's top-ranked bowler.

Below: The world's number one-ranked batsman Virat Kohli of India will be the most-prized scalp for all bowlers at the ICC Cricket World Cup 2019.

Player Rankings: Batsmen Top 30
(as of 3 February 2019)

1 **Virat Kohli** (India)
2 **Rohit Sharma** (India)
3 **Ross Taylor** (New Zealand)
4 **Joe Root** (England)
5 **Babar Azam** (Pakistan)
6 **Francois du Plessis** (South Africa)
7 **Shai Hope** (Windies)
8 **Quinton de Kock** (South Africa)
9 **Fakhar Zaman** (Pakistan)
10 **Shikhar Dhawan** (India)
11 **Kane Williamson** (New Zealand)
12 **Jonny Bairstow** (England)
13 **Hashim Amla** (South Africa)
14 **Tamim Iqbal** (Bangladesh)
15 **Mushfiqur Rahim** (Bangladesh)
16 **Imam-ul-Haq** (Pakistan)
17 **MS Dhoni** (India)
18 **Jos Buttler** (England)
19 **Martin Guptill** (New Zealand)
20 **Eoin Morgan** (England)
21 **Aaron Finch** (Australia)
22 **Kyle Coetzer** (Scotland)
23 **Jason Roy** (England)
24 **Niroshan Dickwella** (Sri Lanka)
25 **Travis Head** (Australia)
26 **Ben Stokes** (England)
27 **David Miller** (South Africa)
28 **Alex Hales** (England)
29 **Angelo Mathews** (Sri Lanka)
30 **Glenn Maxwell** (Australia)

Player Rankings: Bowlers Top 30
(as of 3 February 2019)

1 **Jasprit Bumrah** (India)
2 **Rashid Khan** (Afghanistan)
3 **Trent Boult** (New Zealand)
4 **Kuldeep Yadav** (India)
5 **Yuzvendra Chahal** (India)
6 **Mustafizur Rahman** (Bangladesh)
7 **Kagiso Rabada** (South Africa)
8 **Adil Rashid** (England)
9 **Mujeeb Zadran** (Afghanistan)
10 **Josh Hazlewood** (Australia)
11 **Imran Tahir** (South Africa)
12 **Chris Woakes** (England)
13 **Akila Dananjaya** (Sri Lanka)
14 **Hasan Ali** (Pakistan)
15 **Mohammad Nabi** (Afghanistan)
16 **Dale Steyn** (South Africa)
17 **Bhuvneshwar Kumar** (India)
18 **Mitchell Starc** (Australia)
19 **Andile Phehlukwayo** (South Africa)
20 **Pat Cummins** (Australia)
21 **Tim Murtagh** (Ireland)
22 **Moeen Ali** (England)
23 **Matt Henry** (New Zealand)
24 **Shadab Khan** (Pakistan)
25 **Mashrafe Mortaza** (Bangladesh)
26 **Mitchell Santner** (New Zealand)
27 **Shakib Al Hasan** (Bangladesh)
28 **Mehedi Hasan** (Bangladesh)
29 **Liam Plunkett** (England)
30 **Mohammad Shami** (India)

MEET THE TEAMS

Ten countries will be vying for the biggest prize in one-day cricket in England and Wales in 2019. Seven of those teams – England, Australia, India, New Zealand, Pakistan, Sri Lanka and the Windies – have appeared in all 11 *ICC* Cricket World Cups held to date. South Africa entered the fray in 1992, while Bangladesh joined the party for the first time in 1999. For Afghanistan, this will be their second appearance at the tournament.

Opposite: *Shapoor Zadran celebrates Afghanistan's first-ever victory at the ICC Cricket World Cup, over Scotland at Dunedin in 2015.*

ENGLAND CRICKET

ENGLAND

England have come remarkably close to claiming cricket's biggest prize, reaching the final of the *ICC* Cricket World Cup three times (in 1979, 1987 and 1992), but ended up on the losing side on each of these encounters – indeed, no team has finished as runners-up in the competition on more occasions. However, following a string of dominant performances in the one-day arena in recent times, that have seen them rise to the top of the world rankings, coupled with home advantage, England will justifiably enter the *ICC* Cricket World Cup 2019 as pre-tournament favourites.

NOT THAT ENGLAND made home advantage count in the tournament's formative years, when the first three editions of the *ICC* Cricket World Cup were staged in England. In 1975, they won all three of their group matches in comprehensive fashion, but then came unstuck in a dramatic way against Australia in the semi-final at Headingley. Batting first in swing-and-seam friendly conditions, they crashed to 93 all out (with Gary Gilmour taking 6 for 14 from his 12 overs) and were left to ponder what could have been after Australia inched their way to the total for the loss of six wickets.

England went one better in 1979, reaching the final against the Windies at Lord's, only to be undone by a combination of brilliant batting (Viv Richards scoring an unbeaten 138) and some fantastic fast bowling to lose by 92 runs. They fell short in 1983 as well,

losing to India by six wickets in a one-sided semi-final at Old Trafford.

Many thought their chances of success would be slim when the tournament transferred to the subcontinent in 1987. But this was an experienced England team and one that contained two masters of batting on the region's slow, low pitches. Graham Gooch, in particular, and Mike Gatting led England to group-stage victories over the Windies (twice) and Sri Lanka (twice) and although suffered a pair of defeats to Pakistan, they did enough to reach the semi-finals. They were magnificent against defending champions India in Mumbai. Gooch (115) starred with the bat as England reached a competitive total of 254 for 6, while off-spinner Eddie Hemmings (4 for 52) and seamer Neil Foster (3 for 47) shone with the ball as India slipped to 219 all out. But then England lost their

Left: Graham Gooch is England's all-time leading run-scorer at the ICC Cricket World Cup, with 897 runs.

TOURNAMENT STATS

World ranking: 1
Overall tournament record: P 72, W 41, L 29, Tied 1, No result 1
CWC best: Runner-up (1979, 1987, 1992)
All-time leading batsman: Graham Gooch (1979–92) – 897 runs
Best batting: 158 – Andrew Strauss v India at Bangalore on 27 Feb 2011
All-time leading bowler: Ian Botham (1979–92) – 30 wickets
Best bowling: 5 for 39 – Vic Marks v Sri Lanka at Taunton on 11 June 1983

nerve in the final. They limited Australia to 253 for 5, and reached 135 for 3 in reply before Gatting (41) succumbed to an ill-advised reverse sweep and England, despite the best efforts of Allan Lamb (45), fell an agonizing eight runs short of their target.

If the 1987 tournament was the one that got away from England, then their 1992 campaign in Australia and New Zealand was the one in which they simply had to hold their hands up and admit that they lost to the better side when it truly mattered. This time England had packed their team with all-rounders, and the selection strategy seemed to have worked after England marched through the group stage (finishing second behind New Zealand in the table) and enjoyed a huge slice of good fortune in the semi-final against South Africa. However, against Pakistan

in the final, they were outgunned by veteran all-rounder Imran Khan (who scored 72 with the bat) and young left-arm fast bowler Wasim Akram (who took two vital wickets in two balls) and slipped to a 22-run defeat.

England suffered three group-stage defeats in 1996 but scraped through to the quarter-finals, only to slip to a five-wicket defeat against Sri Lanka in Faisalabad. But if their performances in 1996 had been disappointing, their showing in the 1999 edition of the tournament was calamitous. From an England perspective, this was a tournament during which they could have taken full advantage of home conditions and made a nation fall in love with the game again. But a string of under-par performances, coupled with a questionable selection strategy, saw them fail to reach the Super Sixes

Below left: Mike Gatting's mastery against spin was one of the main reasons behind England's march to the 1987 ICC Cricket World Cup final.

Below right: Jason Roy has added considerable firepower to the top of England's batting order.

and depart the tournament before it had really begun.

Things barely improved for England in South Africa in 2003, as poor performances, coupled with the decision not to play against Zimbabwe in Harare, meant they failed yet again to qualify for the tournament's latter stages. They fared slightly better in the Caribbean four years later, to qualify for the Super Eight stage, but although they recorded expected victories over Ireland, Bangladesh and the Windies, they lost to Sri Lanka, Australia and South Africa and failed to reach the semi-finals. If the tournament had taught England anything, it was that they no longer dined at the top table when it came to one-day cricket.

So when England, thanks to victories over the Netherlands, India, South Africa and the Windies, finally

made it to the knockout stages of the competition in 2011 (for the first time since 1996) there was cause for cheer. Not that it lasted long: Sri Lanka restricted England to 229 for 6 in Colombo and then knocked them off without losing a wicket. And it was a familiar tale of disappointment in Australia and New Zealand four years later: England lost four of their six group matches, including a demoralizing loss to Bangladesh, failed again to reach the knockout stages and returned home with widespread condemnation for their performances ringing in their ears.

So why the confidence this time around? Because, whisper it gently, this is a different England team. For many, the watershed moment arrived during a 3–2 series defeat to New Zealand in the summer of 2015. England may have lost the series, but they learned much from the way in which the New Zealanders went about their business, and the collective smile each of them had on their face while they were doing it, with each knowing exactly what their role in the team was. It provided England with a blueprint as to how they could play

Above left: Jos Buttler has established himself as one of the most complete batsmen in one-day international cricket.

Above right: Under Eoin Morgan's astute captaincy, England have risen to the top of the ICC's One-Day International rankings.

TEAM STATS
Captain: Eoin Morgan
Coach: Trevor Bayliss
Key players: Jason Roy, Joe Root, Jos Buttler, Ben Stokes, Adil Rashid

Above: Adil Rashid's form with the white ball has made him an integral part of England's one-day side.

them, these batsmen have struck 21 centuries since the start of 2017 and have posted a score in excess of 300 on 18 occasions. Their highest, memorably, came when they racked up a world-record 481 for 6 against Australia at Trent Bridge on 19 June 2018.

England's bowling has been equally efficient, too. Leading the way, and defying his critics in the process, has been leg-spinner Adil Rashid, who has become one of the most effective middle-over bowlers in white-ball cricket and has taken an impressive 68 wickets since the turn of 2017 (only Afghanistan's Rashid Khan, with 91, has taken more). Add Chris Woakes, Liam Plunkett, Ben Stokes and Moeen Ali to the mix and you have a bowling unit capable of limiting the best batting line-ups in the world; all of which provided a platform for its exciting batting unit to go about their business.

So, is England's pre-tournament favouritism justified? Recent form and home advantage suggests so, but their recent reputation has been built on series successes, not on one-off matches, and the last time England played in a tournament, in the *ICC Champions Trophy* in June 2017 (a precursor to the *ICC Cricket World Cup 2019*), things did not turn out so well. As now, they were considered pre-tournament favourites, and again they had home advantage, but after beating Bangladesh (by eight wickets), New Zealand (by 87 runs) and Australia (by six wickets) in the group stage, they came unstuck against Pakistan in the semi-final, played at Cardiff. Batting first, England struggled to cope with a dry, abrasive surface on a pre-used pitch and slipped to 211 all out. Pakistan cruised to the target with 12.5 overs to spare and two wickets down. Everyone connected with the England side will hope history does not repeat itself at the *ICC Cricket World Cup 2019*.

the game and, under the inventive and occasionally inspired leadership of Eoin Morgan, they started to flourish.

Since March 2017, England have racked up some impressive series wins: 3–0 against the Windies in the Caribbean; 2–1 against South Africa in England two months later; 4–1 against Australia in Australia in January 2018; a 5–0 drubbing of an understrength Australia in England in June; a 2–1 series victory over India in England later that year; and, most recently, an away series victory over Sri Lanka. England's last series defeat was in January 2017 – 2–1 against India in India, and this side has not lost a home series since 2015 (3–2 against Australia), but they lost a one-off ODI against Scotland in Edinburgh.

So what has been the key to this success? An explosive top order, led by Surrey's Jason Roy and Yorkshire's Jonny Bairstow, a middle order comprising Joe Root, Eoin Morgan and Ben Stokes who are all capable of adapting their games to suit the situation and, in Jos Buttler, arguably the most exciting and destructive batsman in world cricket. Between

SOUTH AFRICA

South Africa have enjoyed a curious, and from the outside, at least, compelling relationship with the *ICC* Cricket World Cup. The tournament has provided both the team and the country with some memorable highs as well as some devastating lows, and the team's progress at the 2019 event, and the manner in which it attempts to redress some historic cricketing wrongs, will provide one of the tournament's intriguing subplots.

SOUTH AFRICA MADE THEIR FIRST appearance in the tournament at the 1992 edition of the event in Australia and New Zealand. Their appearance was hugely significant both for South Africa as a nation and for world sport as a whole. Having suffered nearly 22 years of sporting isolation as a result of the country's oppressive apartheid policy, South Africa – who had been reminding everyone of their sporting supremacy from the sidelines during their years in the wilderness – finally had a chance to show everyone what they could achieve on the international sporting stage. The rest of the world watched on with curiosity.

And they got off to a flier against Australia in Sydney, with Allan Donald to the fore. The young fast bowler, who had established a fearsome reputation in county cricket with Warwickshire, took 3 for 34 in 10 fiery overs to help restrict the home side and defending champions to 170 for 9 off 49 overs, before captain Kepler Wessels hit an unbeaten 81 to lead South Africa to an eye-catching nine-wicket victory.

They slipped up against an impressive New Zealand side in their second match in Auckland, losing by seven wickets, and again against Sri Lanka in their second match, but bounced back with a comfortable 64-run victory against the Windies, with Meyrick Pringle taking 4 for 11. Subsequent victories over Pakistan (by 20 runs), Zimbabwe (by seven wickets) and India (by six wickets) were enough to see them through to the semi-finals.

Above left: Jonty Rhodes' electric performances in the field are one of the abiding memories of the 1992 ICC Cricket World Cup.

Below: South Africa snatched defeat from the jaws of what would have been a famous victory in their 1999 ICC Cricket World Cup semi-final against Australia.

TOURNAMENT STATS

World ranking: 4
Overall tournament record: P 55, W 35, L 18, Tied 2, No result 0
CWC best: Semi-finals (1992, 1999, 2007, 2015)
All-time leading batsman: AB de Villiers (2007–15) – 1,207 runs
Best batting: 188 not out – Gary Kirsten v UAE at Rawalpindi on 16 February 1996
All-time leading bowler: Allan Donald (1992–2003) – 38 wickets
Best bowling: 5 for 18 – Andrew Hall v England at Bridgetown, Barbados, on 17 April 2007

And that is where South Africa experienced *ICC* Cricket World Cup heartbreak for the first time. England batted first and scored 252 for 6 off their 45 overs, the innings curtailed because South Africa had bowled their overs too slowly. South Africa's chase started well, but then they lost their way, slipping to 176 for 5 before Jonty Rhodes (43) got them back on course. With five overs remaining, they needed 45 to win, and that had been reduced to 23 from 13 balls when rain forced the players from the pitch. Crucially, the tournament's rain rules meant that any time lost would result in overs being deducted and that those would be the least productive overs from the side who had batted. The upshot of it all was that when play finally resumed, South Africa's revised target was, farcically, 23 runs from one ball. England went through to the final, the rain rule, mercifully, was scrapped and South Africa were left to lick their wounds wondering what might have been.

They travelled to the subcontinent for the 1996 *ICC* Cricket World Cup determined to right the wrongs of the previous tournament, but few gave them a chance, thinking the slow, low pitches of India and Pakistan would offer little to their pace attack. And so it proved: there were plenty of bright spots, such as Gary Kirsten's glittering unbeaten 188 against the UAE in Rawalpindi and a comfortable 73-run "revenge" victory over England, but they lost their nerve in the quarter-final against the Windies in Karachi,

losing six wickets for 45 runs chasing 265 for victory and ending up 20 runs short.

The 1999 tournament represented South Africa's second brush with *ICC* Cricket World Cup heartbreak – but this time it was all of their own making. Things had started so well for them as they recorded impressive victories over India (by four wickets), Sri Lanka (by 89 runs), England (by 112 runs) and Kenya (by seven wickets) and they could afford to brush off a surprise 48-run defeat to Zimbabwe to qualify, comfortably, for the Super Sixes. There, victories over Pakistan (by three wickets) and New Zealand (by 74

Right: Hashim Amla lies third on South Africa's all-time run-scoring list in one-day internationals with nearly 8,000 runs.

runs) were enough to see them qualify for the semi-finals, where they would play Australia.

The semi-final clash between South Africa and Australia at Edgbaston will live long in the memory – and for all the wrong reasons for South Africa fans. They flourished with the ball, as Shaun Pollock (5 for 36) and Allan Donald (4 for 32) combined to dismiss Australia for 213. South Africa set off in pursuit of the modest target and seemed to be frustrated by the brilliance of Shane Warne (4 for 29), but the match came down to South Africa, with one wicket remaining, needing one run off the last three balls to win. Extraordinarily, they messed it up: Donald was run out, the match ended in a tie and Australia advanced to the final by dint of having a superior tournament run-rate. No one who saw it will ever forget.

So the 2003 tournament, in which the majority of matches were played in South Africa, presented them with a fabulous chance of redemption; an opportunity to lay the "chokers" tag to rest once and for all. But things did not work out as planned. The signs that all might not be well with the team were apparent from their opening match against the Windies. Brian Lara hit a wonderful 116 as the Windies reached 278 for 5 and South Africa's reply fell short by four runs. As expected they beat Kenya, Bangladesh and Canada, but a further defeat to New Zealand left them needing to beat Sri Lanka to advance to the Super Sixes. Sri Lanka scored 268 and South Africa reached 229 for 6 off 45

overs before the rains came to end the match. Amazingly, the Duckworth-Lewis method used to decide weather-affected matches calculated that the match had ended in a tie. Sri Lanka advanced to the Super Sixes, while South Africa exited from their own tournament, cursing the rain gods once again.

They entered the 2007 tournament as the No.1 ranked one-day side in the world and qualified for the Super Eights thanks to victories over the Netherlands (by 221 runs) and Scotland (by seven wickets), although they did suffer an 83-run defeat to Australia. Subsequent victories over Sri Lanka, Ireland and the Windies were enough to see them progress to their third *ICC* Cricket World Cup semi-final, although defeats to Bangladesh (by 67 runs) and New Zealand (by five wickets) revealed a frailty in their batting. Australia exposed it brutally in the semi-finals, dismissing them for 149 and reaching the paltry target for the loss of just three wickets with 18.3 overs to spare.

Not many people fancied South Africa's chances when the tournament

Below: Faf du Plessis has proved to be an inspirational choice as captain for South Africa in all forms of the game.

TEAM STATS
Captain: Faf du Plessis
Coach: Ottis Gibson
Key players: Hashim Amla, Faf du Plessis, JP Duminy, Kagiso Rabada, Dale Steyn

Above left: JP Duminy's contributions with both ball and bat are vital to this South Africa side.

Above right: Veteran fast bowler Dale Steyn's fitness will be crucial for South Africa's hopes at the 2019 ICC Cricket World Cup.

returned to the subcontinent in 2011, and they surprised everyone when they won five of their six matches (losing only to England) to top the Group A table. But they were outgunned by New Zealand in the quarter-final in Dhaka. Batting first, New Zealand limped to 221 for 8, but then dismissed South Africa for 172.

On the face of it, the conditions for the 2015 tournament in Australia and New Zealand seemed more suited to South Africa. And it showed when they won four of six group matches to qualify for the quarter-finals. They brushed aside Sri Lanka in Sydney, bowling them out for 133 and reaching the target in just 18 overs to reach the semi-finals for the fourth occasion, this time against New Zealand in Auckland. Nobody could accuse them of freezing on this occasion: South Africa batted first and reached 281 for 5 in an innings reduced to 43 overs by rain. When the skies cleared, New Zealand were set a revised target of 298 off 43 overs and, spectacularly, they reached it with one ball to spare. No one could deny that that the better team had won.

So what of South Africa's chances for 2019? Will this be the tournament in which they finally lay their *ICC Cricket World Cup* ghosts to rest? It is difficult to find a solid argument for them, as this is a team in flux. There's no AB de Villiers in the batting line-up, Morne Morkel has joined him in international cricket retirement and fast-bowling spearhead Dale Steyn has been troubled by injury. The hugely experienced Hashim Amla and captain Faf du Plessis are the mainstays of the batting line-up, while young tyro Kagiso Rabada leads an exciting but inexperienced bowling attack – one that is prone to inconsistency.

That inconsistency has showed in South Africa's recent results: they have recorded impressive series victories in New Zealand (3–2) and Sri Lanka (3–1), but defeats to England (2–1) and, more significantly, India at home (4–1) in February 2018 suggest that South Africa are some way off one-day cricket's current leading lights. This is a side capable of beating any other on its day, but *ICC* Cricket World Cup success in 2019 may well be beyond them.

INDIA

Two-time tournament winners India will arrive at the 2019 edition of the *ICC* Cricket World Cup as the best supported team in world cricket and as one of the most-fancied teams in the competition, but they have not always had a love affair with the *ICC* Cricket World Cup.

THEY PRODUCED A BIZARRE performance in the very first *ICC* Cricket World Cup match, against England at Lord's on 7 June 1975. After England had reached a then-world record one-day score of 334 for 4 off 60 overs, India produced a torturous, and baffling, reply, limping to 132 for 3 off their 60 overs with opener Sunil Gavaskar – reportedly believing the target to be unobtainable and so using the time at the crease as practice – hitting an unbeaten 36 off 174 balls. India lost the match by 202 runs – and also lost a lot of support in the process. They cruised to a ten-wicket victory over East Africa in their second match and then faced New Zealand at Old Trafford in their final group game needing to win to progress to the semi-finals. India won the toss, batted first and, stifled by the Hadlee brothers (Dayle and Richard) were bowled out for an under-par 230. Glenn Turner hit an unbeaten 114 to guide New Zealand to victory and India's first encounter with the *ICC* Cricket World Cup came to a disappointing close.

But that was nothing compared to their performances in 1979, as India had a tournament to forget, losing

Left: Sunil Gavaskar was India's leading batsman in their early forays at the ICC Cricket World Cup.

Below left: All-rounder Kapil Dev produced some scintillating performances with both bat and ball when India claimed the 1983 ICC Cricket World Cup crown.

TOURNAMENT STATS

World ranking: 2
Overall tournament record: P 75, W 46, L 27, Tied 1, No result 1
CWC best: Champions (1983, 2011)
All-time leading batsman: Sachin Tendulkar (1992–2011) – 2,278 runs
Best batting: 183 – Saurav Ganguly v Sri Lanka at Taunton on 26 May 1999
All-time leading bowler: Javagal Srinath (1992–2003) and Zaheer Khan (2003–11) – 44 wickets
Best bowling: 6 for 23 – Ashish Nehra v England at Durban on 26 February 2003

all three of their matches – against the Windies (by nine wickets), New Zealand (by eight wickets) and, worst of all, against Sri Lanka (by 47 runs). To add to the embarrassment, this was before Sri Lanka had been granted Test status.

All of which meant that very few people thought that India had any chance of winning the trophy when the *ICC* Cricket World Cup returned to British shores in 1983, including many of the Indian players themselves. As one former India player suggested, the players were keener to take in the sights and sounds of London than to play cricket. But that all changed when they produced a mesmerizing performance in their first match,

Below: Sachin Tendulkar appeared in six ICC Cricket World Cups for India and scored an Indian record 2,278 runs in the competition.

against defending champions Windies, who had never lost a match at the *ICC* Cricket World Cup, at Old Trafford. India reached 262 for 8 and then reduced the Windies to 157 for 9 before finally bowling them out for 228. The unexpected, but much-deserved, win was a catalyst for even greater things to come. India beat Zimbabwe in their next game (by five wickets), then lost two on the bounce (against Australia and in the reverse tie against the Windies), but recorded two victories in their final group matches (notably against Australia at Chelmsford) to qualify for the semi-final.

They played England at Old Trafford for a place in the final and utterly dominated them, bowling them out for 213 and reaching the target for the loss of four wickets with 5.2 overs to spare. But the general consensus was that they would have to take their game to another level if they were to stand any chance of beating the Windies in the final. It did not seem as though they could. Batting first, they posted an underwhelming 183 and needed to produce a monumental effort with the ball to have any chance of victory. They did just that: Madan Lal wreaked havoc in the Windies top order, dismissing Desmond Haynes, Viv Richards and Larry Gomes to take 3 for 31, while Mohinder Armanath (3 for 12) ripped through the tail to dismiss the men from the Caribbean for 140. India had become the most unlikely world champions, and a

TEAM STATS
Captain: Virat Kohli
Coach: Ravi Shastri
Key players: Virat Kohli, Rohit Sharma,
MS Dhoni, Jasprit Bumrah,
Bhuvneshwar Kumar

billion diehard cricket fans celebrated back home in India.

So imagine the fervour when the tournament shifted to India and Pakistan in 1987. It was dampened somewhat when India lost their opening match against Australia in Chennai. Australia batted first and posted 270 for 6: initially, everyone thought they had scored 268, before India captain Kapil Dev, sportingly, persuaded the umpires that a Dean Jones four had, in fact, been a six, and the Australian score was increased by two. No one thought it was significant when India raced to 223 for 3 in reply, but they lost their last seven wickets for 46 runs and went on to lose the match by

one run. They recovered well, however, winning the next five of their group matches (including a comprehensive return victory over Australia in Delhi) to reach the semi-finals, where they would face England in Mumbai. Graham Gooch (115) starred for England as they reached 254 for 6 and India's reply never really got going. Mohammad Azharuddin hit an entertaining 64, but his dismissal signalled the end of India's hopes and they collapsed to 219 all out and defeat.

India's performance at the 1992 tournament was calamitous. They beat Pakistan (by 43 runs) and Zimbabwe (by 55 runs), but lost their five other matches and failed to qualify for the semi-finals by some distance – only Sri Lanka and Zimbabwe were below them in the points table.

A return to the subcontinent in 1996 triggered an upturn in performance. True, they suffered group-stage defeats to Australia (by 16 runs) and the tournament's surprise package

Below left: Virat Kohli is widely thought to be the world's best batsman in all formats of the game.

Below: Left-arm leg-spinner Kuldeep Yadav has taken 118 wickets in one-day internationals since the start of 2017.

Sri Lanka (by six wickets) but they won their remaining group matches to qualify for the quarter-finals, where they would play Pakistan in Bangalore. A blistering 97 from Navjot Sidhu led them to a commanding total of 287 for 8, which proved too much for Pakistan, who reached 248 for 9 in reply. India's reward was a semi-final match-up against Sri Lanka at Eden Gardens, Calcutta.

When Sri Lanka slipped to 1 for 2, it seemed as though this was going to be India's day, but Sri Lanka recovered to 251 for 8 and when India slipped to 120 for 8 in reply, their fervent fans had seen enough. Riots broke out in the stands, the match was brought to a premature close and Sri Lanka were awarded the victory by default. It was a dark day for Indian cricket.

The 1999 tournament proved another to forget for India. They did qualify for the Super Sixes, thanks to victories over Kenya, Sri Lanka and England, but then won only one match, against Pakistan at Old Trafford, to finish bottom of the table.

Sachin Tendulkar was their star in South Africa in 2003. The right-hand maestro ended up as the tournament's leading run-scorer (with 673 runs) as India finished second in their group (behind Australia), won all of their Super Sixes matches and brushed off the challenge of Kenya in the semi-finals to reach their second *ICC Cricket World Cup* final. Australia proved too strong for them in Johannesburg, however, reaching 359 for 2 before bowling India out for 234.

They failed spectacularly in the Caribbean four years later, winning only one of their group matches and failing to reach the Super Eights. So the pressure was well and truly on them when the tournament returned to the subcontinent in 2011. They won their opening match against Bangladesh in Dhaka by 87

runs and bar the minor hICCup of a three-wicket defeat to South Africa in Nagpur, looked the team to beat in the tournament. They confirmed that perception with a comfortable five-wicket victory over Australia in the quarter-final and then beat Pakistan by 29 runs in the semi-final to progress to the final in Mumbai. Mahela Jayawardene struck a fine unbeaten 103 to guide Sri Lanka to 274 for 6, before first Gautam Gambhir (97) and then MS Dhoni (91 not out) held their nerve to steer India to victory with eight balls remaining. The tournament's best team had become world champions for the second time.

They made a valiant defence of their crown in Australia and New Zealand in 2015, proving to everyone that this India side was a mature, balanced one, and, most importantly, one that could challenge on any surface. They finished top of their pool, winning all six matches and then beat Bangladesh in the quarter-finals (by 109 runs) before losing to Australia (by 95 runs) in the semi-final. Beaten, yes, but certainly not disgraced.

So, what of the India class of 2019? In Virat Kohli, they possess the finest batsman (in all forms) in world cricket. But he is not alone: add Rohit Sharma, Shikhar Dhawan, Ajinkya Rahane and MS Dhoni to the mix, and you have a batting line-up capable of taking the game away from any opponent. There is plenty of talent in the bowling department, too: Jasprit Bumrah and Bhuvneshwar Kumar have both proved themselves to be fast-medium bowlers of immense quality, while Kuldeep Yadav and Yuzvendra Chahal are both keeping India's rich spin-bowling tradition very much alive. No team will want to face India at the 2019 *ICC Cricket World Cup* – and don't be too surprised if they record a third tournament victory 36 years after their first.

2 MAGIC MOMENTS:
Changing of the guard

The Windies were overwhelming favourites to make it three *ICC* Cricket World Cup wins in a row when they faced India in the final of the *ICC* Cricket World Cup 1983. The men from the Caribbean, champions in 1975 and 1979, had arguably the most feared pace attack world cricket had ever seen, and many thought they would simply prove too strong for India. And so nobody was surprised when India, batting first, slumped to 183 all out in 54.4 overs. But India were following their own script, and what followed was among the most significant few hours in cricket's long history. Led by Mohinder Armanath (3 for 12) and Madan Lal (3 for 31), the Windies collapsed to 140 all out. The Windies' veneer of invincibility had finally cracked but, more significantly, India, the most-supported team in cricket, had become champions of the world. Who knows where the game would be today if they hadn't.

Opposite: *A phenomenal performance from India's bowlers secures the country's first ICC Cricket World Cup title, sparking wild celebrations and a pitch invasion from fans.*

AUSTRALIA

It has been a difficult 12 months for Australian cricket, but the five-time winners have enjoyed a multitude of memorable moments at the ICC Cricket World Cup, and the 2019 tournament could well provide them with a much-needed fillip.

THEY VERY NEARLY WON the inaugural tournament in 1975, showing their intent in the opening match against Pakistan at Headingley, scoring 278 for 7, then dismissing Pakistan for 205. They beat Sri Lanka by 52 runs to book a semi-finals place, but came unstuck against the Windies in their final group match. Australia, batting first, slipped to 192 all out and the Windies cantered to victory for the loss of just three wickets. Defeat meant Australia faced England at Headingley – where their fast bowlers had prospered against Pakistan. They prospered again, this time Gary Gilmour (6 for 14) causing the damage as England collapsed to 93 all out. Australia struggled in reply, but they inched over the winning line for the loss of six wickets to face the Windies in the final.

They made a real fight of it at Lord's. Batting first, the Windies posted a seemingly unassailable 291 for 8; hindered by three run-outs, Australia's reply never really got going, but they fell only 17 runs short of their target.

That was as good as it got for Australia for a while, however. In 1979, with many of their star players sidelines, the team stuggled. They lost their opening match against England at Lord's (by six wickets), slipped to an 89-run defeat against Pakistan at Trent Bridge and, with a semi-final place already out of their reach, recorded their only victory in the competition – a thumping seven-wicket romp over minnows Canada.

Their performances in the 1983 tournament were all the more disappointing because, this time, it was a full-strength Australia side that took to the field. Signs that all was not well with this Australia side surfaced when they lost their opening match of the tournament, to Zimbabwe at Trent Bridge. Batting first, Zimbabwe, playing in their first-ever international match, reached a respectable 239 for 6. The target proved too much for Australia, who could only muster 226 for 7 in reply. They had been on the wrong end of the biggest shock the *ICC* Cricket

Left: Allan Border led Australia to ICC Cricket World Cup glory in 1987.

TOURNAMENT STATS

World ranking: 6
Overall tournament record: P 84, W 62, L 20, Tied 1, No result 1
CWC best: Champions (1987, 1999, 2003, 2007, 2015)
All-time leading batsman: Ricky Ponting (1996–2011) – 1,743 runs
Best batting: 178 – David Warner v Afghanistan at Perth on 4 March 2015
All-time leading bowler: Glenn McGrath (1996–2007) – 71 wickets
Best bowling: 7 for 15 – Glenn McGrath v Namibia at Potcheefstroom on 27 February 2003

World Cup had produced to date – and never recovered. They were thumped by the Windies at Headingley (losing by 101 runs), produced their best performance of the tournament to beat eventual champions India (winning by a mighty 162 runs), gained some measure of

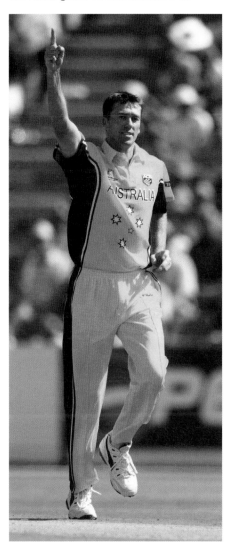

revenge over Zimbabwe (winning by 32 runs), but then suffered further defeats to the Windies and India to miss out on a place in the semi-finals.

The introspection that followed Australia's chastening performances at the 1983 *ICC* Cricket World Cup led to a complete change in approach. And it was a different Australia that arrived in the subcontinent for the 1987 edition of the event. They got off to the best possible start, beating India by one run in Chennai, and followed it up with confidence-boosting victories over Zimbabwe and New Zealand. True, they did lose to India in the two sides' return match in Delhi (by 56 runs), but further wins over Zimbabwe and New Zealand saw them qualify for the semi-finals (for the first time since 1975) with ease. It would be no easy task, however: Australia had to travel to Lahore to take on Pakistan on their home turf. Australia posted 267 for 8 and then

Right: Glenn McGrath took 71 wickets for Australia in four ICC Cricket World Cups between 1996 and 2007.

Far right: Ricky Ponting led from the front for Australia during their march to the ICC Cricket World Cup crown in 2003.

Craig McDermott (5 for 44) shone with ball, ripping through the Pakistan tail as they fell 18 runs short. The final between Australia and England was the most closely contested *ICC* Cricket World Cup final to date. David Boon (75) shone again with the bat as Australia reached 253 for 5, and although England seemed on course for victory, Australia held their nerve when their opponents did not, and won by seven runs.

All of which made their performances at the 1992 event, for which they were co-hosts, all the more disappointing. An opening 37-run defeat against New Zealand in Auckland was surprising, but alarm bells started to ring when they then suffered a thumping nine-wicket reverse against South Africa. Australia recovered to win four matches, but further defeats against England and

Pakistan saw them miss the semi-finals.

A return to the subcontinent in 1996 saw them finish second in their group, with three wins and two defeats, and they eased to victory over New Zealand in the quarter-finals. In their semi-final against the Windies in Mohali, they slipped to 15 for 4 before Stuart Law (72) and Michael Bevan (69) lifted them to 207 for 8. The Windies reached 165 for 2 in reply, but lost their last eight wickets for 37 runs to hand Australia a five-run victory and a place in the final against Sri Lanka. Batting first, Australia posted 241 for 7, but Sri Lanka replied magnificently. Aravinda da Silva (107 not out) led the way as Sri Lanka raced to the target for the loss of only three wickets.

They suffered two group-stage defeats in 1999 (to New Zealand and Pakistan) but still qualified for the Super Sixes, at which point they came alive. They won their three matches to reach the last four and enjoyed a huge slice of luck to win their semi-final against South Africa. Against Pakistan in the final at Lord's, luck did not enter the equation. Australia were simply magnificent as Shane Warne took 4 for

Above left: Adam Gilchrist hit a sparkling 149 in the 2007 ICC Cricket World Cup final as Australia beat Sri Lanka.

Above right: Steve Smith is one of the world's top batsmen in every form of cricket.

TEAM STATS

Captain: Tim Paine
Coach: Justin Langer
Key players: Aaron Finch, Steve Smith, Glenn Maxwell, Mitchell Starc, Josh Hazelwood

Above: *Josh Hazelwood will lead Australia's three-pronged pace attack at the 2019 ICC Cricket World Cup.*

33 and Pakistan slipped to 132 all out. Australia reached the target in 20.1 overs to become world champions for the second time.

As impressive as they had been in 1999, Australia were totally dominant in South Africa in 2003. Their team, with potential match-winners everywhere in their line-up, left their rivals trailing in their wake. They won all 10 of their matches, including a 125-run victory over India in the final in Johannesburg. Ricky Ponting scored 140 not out and Glenn McGrath took three wickets as Australia became the first team since the Windies in 1979 to retain their *ICC Cricket World Cup* crown.

Australia were just as good in the Caribbean four years later. Once again, they won all their matches in the group and Super Eight stages. They outplayed South Africa in the semi-final, bowling them out for 149 and reaching the target with 18.3 overs to spare. And they were similarly dominant against Sri Lanka in the rain-affected final. Australia, batting first, reached 281 for 4 off 38 overs, with Adam Gilchrist hammering 149. Sri Lanka, chasing a revised target of 269 from 36 overs, never came close,

reaching 215 for 8. Australia had made history by winning three consecutive *ICC* Cricket World Cups.

The run came to an end in the subcontinent in 2011, when they lost to India by five wickets in the quarter-final, but they were back on track again in 2015, when the tournament returned to Australia and New Zealand. They lost a thrilling match against New Zealand in the group stages (by one wicket in Auckland), but still qualified for the knockout stages with ease. They brushed aside Pakistan in the quarter-finals (by six wickets) and proved too strong for India in the semi-finals (winning by 95 runs) to set up a final showdown against New Zealand – the only side to have beaten them in the tournament. They set the record straight this time round, though, bowling out New Zealand for 183 and reaching the target for the loss of just three wickets with 16.5 overs to spare. It was their fourth *ICC* Cricket World Cup success in five tournaments – a period of unprecedented success.

But all has not been well with Australian cricket in recent times. Big name stars, such as Michael Clarke and Mitchell Johnson have retired and their replacements have taken time to bed in. Nonetheless, Australia will see the 2019 *ICC* Cricket World Cup as an occasion in which they can put themselves back on track – and they certainly have the talent at their disposal to do it. Steve Smith will be back in the fold and, in Aaron Finch, Travis Head and Glenn Maxwell, they have three batsmen capable of match-winning feats. Concerns will be about the fitness of their bowling attack, notably Mitchell Starc, Pat Cummins and Josh Hazelwood – if these three are fit and firing, Australia will cause problems to any opponent. Even though this is a team that has won only six of their last 25 one-day internationals, people should only dismiss Australia's 2019 *ICC* Cricket World Cup ambitions at their peril.

NEW ZEALAND
=======

Six-time semi-finalists and runners-up in 2015, New Zealand have consistently overachieved at the *ICC* Cricket World Cup. And with a collection of match-winners among their ranks, there is no reason why they cannot spring a few surprises at the 2019 tournament.

THE SIGNS THAT NEW ZEALAND were prepared to battle for all their worth were there from their very first appearance at the *ICC* Cricket World Cup, in England in 1975. They won their opening match, against East Africa, by the comprehensive margin of 181 runs, after Glenn Turner had struck a magnificent unbeaten 171 (at the time, the highest score in one-day international history). They lost to England in their second match, mainly as a result of electing to field rather than bat after winning the toss, which set up a showdown against India at Old Trafford to decide who would join England in the semi-finals. India batted first and were bowled out for 230; Glenn Turner scored his second century in three matches (114 not out) to guide his side to a four-wicket victory with seven balls to spare and a last-four clash against the Windies at The Oval. They could not cope with the Windies' fearsome pace attack, however, and slipped to 158 all out.

The Windies reached the target for the loss of five wickets – New Zealand had been beaten, but they had certainly not been disgraced.

It was more of the same in 1979. They won their opening match against Sri Lanka at Trent Bridge by nine wickets, beat India by eight wickets at Headingley and then, with a semi-final place already assured, faced the Windies at Trent Bridge. They made a better fight of it on this occasion, restricting the reigning champions to 244 for 7, but again found the Windies pace attack too hot to handle, and

Above left: Martin Crowe was the leading batsman at the 1992 ICC Cricket World Cup.

Below: Stephen Fleming led New Zealand to the semi-finals at the 1999 ICC Cricket World Cup.

TOURNAMENT STATS

World ranking: 3
Overall tournament record: P 79, W 48, L 30, Tied 0, No result 1
CWC best: Runners-up (2015)
All-time leading batsman: Stephen Fleming (1996–2007) – 1,075 runs
Best batting: 237 not out – Martin Guptill v Windies at Wellington on 21 March 2015
All-time leading bowler: Jacob Oram (2003–11) and Daniel Vettori (2003–15) – 36 wickets
Best bowling: 7 for 33 – Tim Southee v England at Wellington on 20 February 2015

could only reach 212 for 9 in reply. They ran England close in the semi-final, too, restricting the tournament hosts to 221 for 8, but yet again they could not get over the winning line: they could only manage 212 for 9 to fall ten runs short of victory. Had New Zealand overachieved by reaching two successive semi-finals, or had they simply played to their natural level – a couple of notches below the very best teams in one-day cricket?

It seemed as though it might be the former following New Zealand's performances at the 1983 tournament. England hammered them in their opening match at The Oval, reaching 322 for 6 and then bowling them out for 216 to inflict a morale-sapping 106-run defeat. They needed to bounce back quickly in their second match, against Pakistan at Edgbaston, and did. Batting first, they reached 238 for 9 and then dismissed Pakistan for 186, with Richard Hadlee and Jeremy Coney taking three wickets apiece. They beat Sri Lanka too, to place themselves firmly in contention for a semi-final spot at the group's halfway stage. But then they fell apart, losing to Sri Lanka, England and, crucially, to Pakistan, who qualified for the semi-finals at their expense by dint of a superior tournament run-rate.

A shift to the subcontinent for the 1987 tournament did not coincide with an upturn in fortune or form for New Zealand. They beat Zimbabwe twice, but lost all four of their matches against India and Australia to finish third in their group – some 12 points

behind second-placed Australia.

They were arguably the team of the tournament in 1992, however, when the *ICC* Cricket World Cup descended on Australia and New Zealand. They kicked off their campaign with a surprise 37-run victory over Australia in Auckland, with Martin Crowe (100 not out) the hero. And, revelling in home conditions, the wins kept on coming: seven of them, with their only defeat coming against Pakistan in Christchurch. People were starting

Right: It was semi-final heartbreak for New Zealand once again in 2011, when they lost to Sri Lanka in Colombo.

to talk up New Zealand's chances of winning the tournament, but, for the third time in their history, their dreams came to an end in the semi-finals. Pakistan were the villains on this occasion. New Zealand batted first in Auckland and reached 262 for 7. But it wasn't enough. Pakistan, led by Inzamam-ul-Haq (60) and Javed Miandad (57) reached the target with an over to spare.

They recorded group-stage victories over England, the UAE and the Netherlands to qualify for the tournament's knockout stages in 1996, but then ran into Australia in the quarter-finals at Chennai. Batting first, New Zealand posted a challenging 286 for 9 (Chris Harris top-scoring with 130), but Australia made light work of the target. Mark Waugh hit an effortless 110 as Australia eased over the winning line for the loss of just four wickets with 2.1 overs to spare.

New Zealand produced a series of up-and-down performances in 1999. They edged through the group stage on run-rate (marginally ahead of the Windies) and again through the Super Sixes, again on run-rate (this time at Zimbabwe's expense). But the upshot of it all was that they scraped through to the semi-finals (their fourth) to play Pakistan, the team who had ended their dreams in 1992. New Zealand batted first and posted 241 for 7; Pakistan then reached the target in emphatic fashion – losing only one wicket with 2.3 overs to spare.

In 2003, New Zealand fell foul of politics. During the group stages, they had taken the decision not to travel to Nairobi to play Kenya due to security concerns. Kenya had been awarded the victory. New Zealand qualified for the Super Sixes along with Kenya – with the sides keeping any points they had gained against fellow qualifiers from their group. New Zealand had lost to both Sri Lanka and Kenya, so carried no points forward. They did beat Zimbabwe in the Super Sixes, but defeats to India and Australia cost them a place in the semi-finals – and how they must have rued the points they "lost" against Kenya.

It was a familiar tale in the Caribbean in 2007. New Zealand finished top of their group thanks to victories over England, Kenya and Canada. They then won four of their six matches in the Super Eights to qualify for the semi-finals – for the fifth time in their history. Could they finally break the jinx? This time Sri Lanka were the team to end the dream. Batting first, Sri Lanka posted 289 for 5; New Zealand's reply never got going and they slipped to 208 all out in the 42nd over.

The pattern was becoming familiar,

Below: Captain Kane Williamson is considered to be among the big four of batsmen in world cricket.

TEAM STATS
Captain: Kane Williamson
Coach: Gary Stead
Key players: Martin Guptill, Kane Williamson, Ross Taylor, Tim Southee, Trent Boult

Above left: Trent Boult shone during the 2015 ICC Cricket World Cup and New Zealand will be hoping for more of the same in England and Wales in 2019.

Above right: Ross Taylor is closing in fast on Stephen Fleming's all-time New Zealand record for the most runs in one-day international cricket.

and it was repeated in 2011. New Zealand won four of their six matches to qualify from Group A. They then beat South Africa by 49 runs in a one-sided quarter-final in Dhaka to earn a place in the last four – against Sri Lanka in Colombo. New Zealand batted first and were dismissed for an under-par 217; Sri Lanka wobbled in reply, but eventually got over the winning line for the loss of five wickets with 2.1 overs to spare. As Thilan Samaraweera hit the winning runs, New Zealand's players sank to their knees in unison.

So it was hard to get too excited for New Zealand after they got off to a blistering start during their 2015 campaign. We had seen it all before. Back in 1992, the last time the tournament had been played in Australia and New Zealand, the New Zealanders had revelled in home conditions only to fall short when it mattered. But when they finished top of their group, with six wins from six, it was hard not to think that this New Zealand side was made of sterner stuff. They brushed aside the Windies in the quarter-finals, winning by 143

runs thanks to Martin Guptill's world-record score of 237 not out – and then faced South Africa, a team who had experienced their own ICC Cricket World Cup nightmares, in the semi-finals. In a fascinating contest, New Zealand won the day, reaching their revised target of 298 from 43 overs off the very last ball of the match. How they celebrated. But perhaps the effort taken to lay to rest their semi-final ghosts had taken too much out of them, for Australia simply outplayed them in the final. New Zealand were bowled out for 183 and Australia reached the target for the loss of only three wickets with 16.5 overs to spare.

Can New Zealand go one better in 2019? The core of the 2015 side remains, and in Martin Guptill, Kane Williamson and Ross Taylor they have three outstanding performers with the bat. Their bowling department, spearheaded by Trent Boult and Tim Southee, should enjoy bowling in English conditions, too. New Zealand's rich history at the ICC Cricket World Cup suggests they will go deep into the tournament, but a ICC Cricket World Cup win might just be beyond them.

3 MAGIC MOMENTS:

Imran's crowning moment

The *ICC* Cricket World Cup 1992 final between Pakistan and England ebbed and flowed in a mesmerizing fashion. Batting first after winning the toss, Pakistan slipped to 24 for 2 before their captain, Imran Khan, playing in his final match, rescued them, crafting a cautious 72 to lead his side to 249 for 6. England slipped to 21 for 2 in reply, but then staged a recovery. Allan Lamb and Neil Fairbrother rallied, before Wasim Akram removed Lamb (31) and Chris Lewis in successive deliveries to hand Pakistan control. Then Fairbrother shepherded the tail to give England renewed hope, but when he fell for 62, England's chance seemed to have gone. Pakistan's moment of glory finally came when, fittingly, Imran claimed England's final wicket (Richard Illingworth). Pakistan had won the World Cup for the first and, to date, only, time in their history – and their captain, Imran Khan, had hauled them over the winning line.

Opposite: Influential both with the bat and the ball, Imran Khan was rightly hailed by teammates, fans, and the entire nation of Pakistan for his performance.

PAKISTAN

Pakistan are the Jeckyll and Hyde of world cricket, and there is no more compelling side to watch. On their day, they can be mesmerizing, a side that is capable of steam rollering any other; but they are equally capable of falling apart in dramatic style and slipping to some unexplainable defeats. The question is, which Pakistan will turn up to the *ICC ICC* Cricket World Cup in 2019?

THEY HAD THEIR FIRST experience of *ICC* Cricket World Cup heartache at the very first edition of the event, in England in 1975. They suffered a comprehensive defeat against Australia in their opening match, bowled out for 205, chasing 279, to lose by 73 runs. That left them needing to beat the Windies, the strong pre-tournament favourites, in their second match at Edgbaston to stand any realistic chance of progressing to the semi-finals. And they came mighty close to pulling off a huge upset. Batting first, they posted a competitive 266 for 7, with captain Majid Khan top-scoring with 60. And when the Windies slipped to 203 for 9 in reply, how they must have sensed glory. But Deryck Murray (60 not out) and Andy Roberts (24 not out) added 64 unlikely runs for the final wicket and the Windies limped over the winning line with two balls to spare. Pakistan were left to ponder what could have been. They did record a thumping 192-run win over Sri Lanka in their final group match, but by then their tournament was already over.

They produced some eye-catching performances at the 1979 tournament. If their opening eight-wicket victory over Canada at Headingley was routine, then their one-sided 89-run win against an albeit understrength Australia at Trent Bridge was not, and although they lost their final group match to England (by 14 runs), they had done enough to reach the semi-finals. Could they down the mighty Windies at The Oval? The men from the Caribbean proved too strong,

Above left: Javed Miandad is Pakistan's all-time leading run-scorer at the *ICC* Cricket World Cup, with 1,083 runs.

Below: Wasim Akram produced a match-turning performance for Pakistan during the 1992 *ICC* Cricket World Cup final against England.

TOURNAMENT STATS

World ranking: 5
Overall tournament record: P 71, W 40, L 29, Tied 0, No result 2
CWC best: Champions (1992)
All-time leading batsman: Javed Miandad (1975–96) – 1,083 runs
Best batting: 160 – Imran Nazir v Zimbabwe at Kingston on 21 March 2011
All-time leading bowler: Wasim Akram (1987–2003) – 55 wickets
Best bowling: 5 for 16 – Shahid Afridi v Kenya at Hambantota on 23 February 2011

scoring 293 for 6 off their 60 overs and bowling out Pakistan for 250.

They produced a mix-and-match set of performances in 1983, winning three and losing two of their opening group matches. It meant that they not only had to beat New Zealand in the final round of group matches, but they also had to score enough runs to better New Zealand's tournament run-rate if they wanted to qualify for the semi-finals. They did both: batting first, Pakistan reached 261 for 3, with Zaheer Abbas hitting an unbeaten 103, and then bowled out New Zealand for 250. They had produced the goods when it mattered, but yet again they faced the giant obstacle of the Windies in the semi-final, again played at The Oval. And, yet again, they came up short. Batting first, Pakistan stumbled to 184 for 8; the Windies romped to the target for the loss of just two wickets with 11.2 overs to spare. And Pakistan's disappointment must have intensified even further when their arch-rivals India went on to topple the Windies in the final to become champions.

Pakistan's hopes must have been high when they co-hosted the 1987 *ICC* Cricket World Cup with India. Would a switch to home turf trigger an upturn in fortune? They were one of the standout teams during the group stages, winning five of their six matches – including a confidence-boosting one-wicket victory over the Windies in Lahore – to qualify for the semi-finals as the leading team in Group B. And when they reached 150 for 3 chasing Australia's total of

267 in the semi-final in Lahore, they must have felt that a place in the *ICC* Cricket World Cup final was firmly within their grasp. However, they lost their last five wickets for just 13 runs and slumped to an 18-run defeat. Their dream of lifting the *ICC* Cricket World Cup on the subcontinent was shattered.

Pakistan brought a blend of wizened internationals and exciting youthful talent to Australia and New Zealand in 1992, for what was to be Imran Khan's final foray in international cricket. But few thought them capable of providing their captain with the send-off he so desperately wanted.

Right: Babar Azam has emerged as one of Pakistan's leading batsmen in recent times.

And they did little during the group stage (in which every side played the other) to dispel that feeling. True, they recorded wins over Zimbabwe, Australia, Sri Lanka and New Zealand, but they also suffered three defeats – to the Windies (by 10 wickets), India (by 43 runs) and South Africa (by 20 runs) and ultimately had the rain to thank for reaching the semi-finals.

When Pakistan played England in Adelaide, they collapsed to 74 all out and seemed destined for defeat before the rain came to save them. The one point they earned from that no-result match was crucial – and they took full advantage of their good fortune. They were magnificent in their semi-final against New Zealand in Auckland, chasing down an imposing target of 263 with an over to spare, with young batsman Inzamam-ul-Haq (60) the star of the show. It was another emerging talent, left-arm fast bowler Wasim Akram, who turned the final in their favour, too. Batting first against England in Melbourne, Pakistan had scored 249 for 6 – Imran top-scoring with a patient 72. England had recovered from 21 for 2 to 141 for 4 in reply, before Wasim took two wickets in two balls. England never recovered, Pakistan went on to win the match by 22 runs and Imran Khan bowed out of international cricket with the game's biggest trophy in his hands.

They made a commendable defence of their crown when the *ICC Cricket World Cup* returned to the subcontinent in 1996, winning four of their five group matches (losing only to South Africa, by five wickets,

in Karachi) to qualify for the quarter-finals – where they would face India in Bangalore. India, batting first, raced to 287 for 8, thanks to Navjot Sidhi's 115-ball 93, and Pakistan, always behind the run-rate, struggled to 248 for 9 in reply. Their reign as world champions was over.

They looked set for a second title in 1999, but fell apart when it mattered. They had impressed during the group stages, winning four of their five matches (their only defeat a surprise reverse against Bangladesh), had finished top of the Super Sixes table and then seen off New Zealand with ease in the semi-finals – by nine wickets, thanks to Saeed Anwar's magnificent unbeaten 113. But they were woeful in the final against Australia. Batting first, they collapsed to 132 all out and Australia raced to the target for the loss of just two wickets with 29.5 overs to spare. It was the most one-sided final in *ICC* Cricket World Cup history.

They had tournaments to forget in 2003 and 2007. In Africa in 2003, they won only two matches (against Namibia and the Netherlands) and

Below: Fakhar Zaman hit a Pakistan record 210 not out against Zimbabwe in Bulaway in July 2018.

TEAM STATS
Captain: Sarfraz Ahmed
Coach: Mickey Arthur
Key players: Babar Azam, Fakhar Zaman, Shoaib Malik, Hasan Ali, Mohammad Amir

Above left: *Mohammad Amir is the spearhead of an impressive Pakistan bowling attack.*

Above right: *Hasan Ali, with 64 one-day international wickets, has been Pakistan's leading bowler since the start of 2017.*

failed to progress beyond the group stages. Things got even worse for them in the Caribbean in 2007. They lost their opening match to the Windies (by 54 runs), suffered a shock defeat to tournament newcomers Ireland (by three wickets) and, with their hopes of reaching the Super Sixes already extinguished, recorded their only victory, against Zimbabwe (by 93 runs), in the final round of group matches.

They fared better when the *ICC* Cricket World Cup returned to the subcontinent in 2011 – even though no matches were played in Pakistan. They were the pick of the teams during the group stages, winning five of their six matches, and thumped the Windies by ten wickets in their quarter-final in Dhaka. But they never really got going against India in the much-hyped semi-final in Chandigarh. Chasing 261 for victory, they were always behind the run-rate and slipped to 231 all out to lose by 29 runs.

It was a similar tale in Australia and New Zealand in 2015. Returning to the scene of their 1992 triumph, they won four out of six matches during the group stage, but their

hopes came to an abrupt end against Australia in the quarter-finals. Batting first in Adelaide, Pakistan found the Australian pace attack too hot to handle and posted an under-par total of 213 all out. It was never going to be enough: Australia raced to the target for the loss of four wickets with 16.1 overs to spare.

So, how to rate Pakistan's chances for 2019? They are currently ranked fifth in the *ICC* World Rankings. In Babar Azam, Fakhar Zaman and the experienced Shoaib Malik, they have a trio of batsmen who have scored heavily in recent times. But it is in the bowling department that their strength truly lies. Fast-medium bower Hasan Ali (with 64 wickets since the turn of 2017) is the pick of the bunch, ably supported by a selection from Mohammad Amir, Junaid Khan, Shadeb Khan and Mohammad Afeez – a combination that, on their day, could unpick the world's best batting line-ups. Expect Pakistan to reach the tournament's knockout stages, but where they go from there very much depends on which Pakistan turns up on the day.

বাংলাদেশ

BANGLADESH

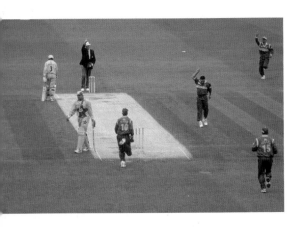

Bangladesh is a country with a population of 164 million people, the majority of whom are diehard cricket fans. And their team's journey towards the top table of international cricket, since the country was granted Test status in 2000, has provided compelling viewing. Initially, they were the push-overs of world cricket, but they have developed into an accomplished side that is more than capable of holding its own against even the world's best teams.

AS AN ASSOCIATE MEMBER of the *ICC*, they watched on in frustration during the first six editions of the *ICC* Cricket World Cup between 1975 and 1996, and only got to experience their first taste of the tournament in 1999. It turned out to be quite an outing, with some disheartening lows and some unbelievable highs. The lows came first. In their first-ever *ICC* Cricket World Cup match, Bangladesh faced New Zealand in Chelmsford. Put into bat, they lost their first wicket to the third ball of the match and never recovered: No. 10 Enamul Haque top-scored with just 19 as Bangladesh slumped to 116 all out and New Zealand reached the target with ease in the 33rd over for the loss of four wickets.

They fared only marginally better in their second match, against the Windies in Dublin. Batting first, Mehrab Hossain top-scored with a patient 64, but only two other batsmen reached double figures and they were dismissed for 182 in the 49th over. The Windies struggled initially

against Bangladesh's bowlers but still reached their target in the 47th over.

If these were expected losses, their third match against fellow qualifiers Scotland in Edinburgh was a must-win affair. Again their batsmen struggled. Batting first, they slipped to 26 for 5 before Minhajul Abedin (68 not out) and Naimur Rahman (36) rallied to lead them to a defendable total of 185 for 9.

Above left: Bangladesh conjured up a memorable victory over Pakistan at the 1999 ICC Cricket World Cup.

Below: Bangladesh's victory over India at the 2007 ICC Cricket World Cup helped them progress beyond the group stage for the first time.

TOURNAMENT STATS

World ranking: 7
Overall tournament record: P 32, W 11, L 20, Tied 0, No result 1
CWC best: Quarter-finals (2015)
All-time leading batsman: Shakib Al Hasan (2007–15) – 540 runs
Best batting: 128 not out – Mahmudullah v New Zealand at Hamilton on 13 March 2015
All-time leading bowler: Shakib Al Hasan (2007–15) – 23 wickets
Best bowling: 4 for 21 – Sahfiul Islam v Ireland at Dhaka on 25 February 2011

Bangladesh's bowlers impressed again as they bowled out Scotland for 163 to record their first *ICC* Cricket World Cup victory. They lost to Australia by seven wickets next, but then played Pakistan at Northampton in what turned out to be an unforgettable match. Bangladesh made 223 for 9 (the first time they had passed 200 in the tournament); Pakistan, in reply, slipped to 42 for 5 and never recovered, ultimately falling for 162. Bangladesh departed the tournament with their heads held high and that victory did much to hasten Bangladesh's elevation to Test status the following year.

The 2003 tournament provided Bangladesh's players with an opportunity to show just how far their cricket had come since becoming a fully-fledged Test team. But the team's

ight: Mahmudullah's nbeaten 128 against ew Zealand was ne of the batting erformances of the 015 ICC Cricket World 'up.

performances generated far more questions than answers. The signs that this was going to be a tournament to forget for Bangladesh were there from their first match against Canada (playing at the tournament for the first time since 1979) at Durban. Canada, batting first, made an under-par 180 all out, but it was too tough a target for Bangladesh, who slumped to a sorry 120 all out to lose by 60 runs. Things did not get any better. They could only manage 124 all out against Sri Lanka in their second match and lost by 10 wickets. Rain saved them against the Windies in Benoni to hand them their first points of the tournament, but they then suffered comprehensive defeats to South Africa (by 10 wickets), New Zealand (seven wickets) and Kenya (by 32 runs) to depart the tournament without a win to their name. The statistics spoke for themselves: they had failed to pass 200 in all five of their completed innings. After all the optimism generated from their performances in 1999, following their dismal showing in 2003, the common question was Bangladesh had been granted Test status too early.

So this was a side with a point to prove when the *ICC* Cricket World Cup reconvened in the Caribbean in 2007. And the team responded in style, producing its best performance at the tournament to date. Their first match provided them with a stern test – against India in Port-of-Spain, Trinidad. India won the toss, batted first and – in the face of some

TEAM STATS

Captain: Mashrafe Mortaza
Coach: Steve Rhodes
Key players: Tamim Iqbal, Mushfiqur Rahim, Mahmudullah, Shakib Al Hasan, Mashrafe Mortaza

impressive fast bowling, notably from Mashrafe Mortaza (4 for 38) – struggled to 191 all out. Bangladesh made hard going of the run-chase, but thanks to half-centuries from Tamim Iqbal (51), Mushfiqur Rahim (56 not out) and Shakib Al Hasan (53), reached the target with nine balls to spare to record a memorable victory. They suffered a comprehensive defeat to Sri Lanka in their second match, losing by 193 runs, but when Sri Lanka then went on to beat India, it meant that if Bangladesh could beat Bermuda in their final group game they would get beyond the competition's group stages for the first time in their history. In a rain-affected match reduced to 21 overs per side, they restricted Bermuda to 94 for 9 and reached their target in the 17th over for the loss of

just three wickets. The Bangladesh dressing room was exultant. They went on to produce another shock, beating South Africa by 67 runs in Georgetown, Guyana, but that proved to be their only victory in the Super Eights. Even so, it was Bangladesh's best showing at the *ICC Cricket World Cup* to date and their naysayers, for the time being at least, had been hushed.

Confidence, therefore, was understandably high when the tournament returned to the subcontinent in 2011, with Bangladesh as joint hosts (with India and Sri Lanka). Could they make home advantage count? They lost their opening match against India in Dhaka by 87 runs and, although they notched up wins against Ireland (by 27 runs), England (by two wickets) and the Netherlands (by six wickets), they suffered further defeats to the Windies and to South Africa to miss out on the quarter-finals. It had to be considered a disappointment that they failed to reach the last eight.

All of which explains why nobody really fancied Bangladesh to do anything at all of note when the

Below left: Mushfiqur Rahim adds a touch of class to Bangladesh's middle-order.

Below right: Shakib Al Hasan has scored more runs and taken more wickets than any other Bangladesh player at the ICC Cricket World Cup.

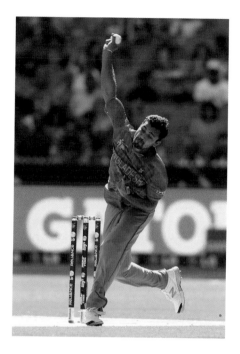

Right: Mashrafe Mortaza is Bangladesh's all-time leading wicket-taker in one-day international cricket with 252 wickets over a 17-year career.

ICC Cricket World Cup moved on to Australia and New Zealand in 2015. The thinking was that if they could not reach the quarter-finals in home conditions, how could they be expected to succeed on the faster, bouncier pitches of Australia and the seam-friendly surfaces of New Zealand? They got off to an encouraging start in their opening match against Afghanistan in Canberra. Mushfiqur Rahim (71) led the way with the bat as Bangladesh posted 267 all out and captain Mushrafe Mortaza (3 for 20) starred with the ball as Afghanistan were bowled out for 162 to hand Bangladesh a confidence-boosting 105-run victory. Their second match, against Australia in Brisbane, was washed out and Bangladesh then slumped to a 92-run defeat against Sri Lanka. It left them needing to win two of their final three group matches to stand any chance of progressing to the quarter-finals. They won the first, against Scotland, by six wickets – but the result does not tell the entire story of the match. Scotland batted first, posted an imposing total of 318 for 8 and must have thought they had a fantastic chance of winning the game. Bangladesh had other ideas. Tamim Iqbal (93) led from the front and his team-mates followed as they raced to the target for the loss of just four wickets with 11 balls to spare. England came next. Bangladesh slipped to 8 for 2 before Mahmudullah (103) and Mushfiqur Rahim (89) led a recovery to take them to 275 for 7. With Jos Buttler (65) at the crease, England seemed on course for victory, but when he fell, England's hopes went with him and Bangladesh edged to a 15-run victory. They lost their final group match against New Zealand (by three wickets) but by then they already had one eye on their quarter-final match. They were no match for India in Melbourne. India batted first and posted 302 for 6; in reply, none of Bangladesh's batsmen could capitalize on good starts (six batsmen passed 20) and they fell to a 109-run defeat. Still, it had been a hugely positive tournament for Bangladesh.

This team are no longer the minnows of world cricket; they have star quality in their ranks. In Tamim Iqbal, Mushfiqur Rahim, Shakib Al Hasan and Mahmudullah, they have four batsmen capable of producing match-winning knocks. They have plenty in their bowling locker, too: Mustafizur Rahman, Mashrafe Mortaza, Shakib Al Hasan and Rubel Hossain have all proved themselves to be fine performers on the international stage. In the last two years, they have recorded impressive victories over Sri Lanka, Pakistan, the Windies and New Zealand, and they reached the semi-finals of the *ICC* Champions Trophy when it was staged in England and Wales in 2017. Bangladesh will be eyeing a *ICC* Cricket World Cup quarter-final place once again in 2019, and this side might just be ready to go even further.

4 MAGIC MOMENTS:

The day of the underdog

Australia were overwhelming favourites to win the final of the *ICC* Cricket World Cup 1996. Led by the Waugh brothers, Mark and Steve, and their talismanic young leg-spinner Shane Warne, they had become the leading side in world cricket: how could Sri Lanka live with them? Comfortably, as it turned out. Sri Lanka's all-out attacking approach had brought them success in the tournament and an inner steel and depth of confidence that everyone underestimated, including the Australians. They restricted Australia to 241 for 7 and even when they slipped to 21 for 2 in reply, they did not panic. Led by Aravinda de Silva (107 not out), Asanka Gurusinha (65) and captain Arjuna Ranatunga (47 not out), they romped to their target with 3.4 overs to spare. They had shocked the world to become the most popular winners in the tournament's history and, more significantly, had forever changed the way one-day cricket was played in the process.

Opposite: Aravinda de Silva moves towards hitting a century for Sri Lanka in the ICC Cricket World Cup 1996 final, on the way to a shock victory over favourites Australia.

SRI LANKA

Sri Lanka have a warm relationship with the *ICC* Cricket World Cup. They were the tournament's fairy-tale champions in 1996, and reached the final in both 2007 and 2011. The question is, how far can this talented group of players go in 2019?

NOT THEN A FULLY-FLEDGED Test cricketing nation, Sri Lanka appeared at the first-ever *ICC* Cricket World Cup in England in 1975. Their first match was against the mighty Windies at Old Trafford, and, predictably, they struggled. Batting first, they slumped to 86 all out and the Windies eased to the target for the loss of just a single wicket. They produced a better showing against Australia in their second match, at The Oval. Australia scored 328 for 5 and although Sri Lanka never threatened the target, they reached a respectable 276 for 4. Pakistan may have outgunned them in their final match at Trent Bridge, winning by 192 runs, but Sri Lanka must have learned a great deal from their first experience of the *ICC* Cricket World Cup.

They travelled to the 1979 *ICC* Cricket World Cup as the best non-Test playing nation. They lost their opening match against New Zealand at Trent Bridge by nine wickets and their match against the Windies was abandoned. But then came their final group match, against India at Old Trafford. Put into bat, Sri Lanka battled their way to 238 for 5 off 60 overs. When India reached 132 for 3 in reply, everyone was

Above left: Arjuna Ranatunga lifts the ICC Cricket World Cup trophy in 1996.

Below left: Aravinda de Silva's nerveless unbeaten 107 guided Sri Lanka to a memorable victory over Australia in the 1996 ICC Cricket World Cup final.

TOURNAMENT STATS

World ranking: 8
Overall tournament record: P 73, W 35, L 35, Tied 1, No result 2
CWC best: Champions (1996)
All-time leading batsman: Kumar Sangakkara (2003–15) – 1,532 runs
Best batting: 161 not out – Tillakaratne Dilshan v Bangladesh at Melbourne on 26 February 2015
All-time leading bowler: Muttiah Muralitharan (1996–2011) – 68 wickets
Best bowling: 6 for 25 – Chaminda Vaas v Bangladesh at Pietermaritzburg on 14 February 2003

expecting an Indian victory. However, they lost their last seven wickets for 59 runs to hand Sri Lanka a richly deserved 47-run victory. It was the first victory an Associate Member team had ever recorded at the *ICC* Cricket World Cup and was a hugely significant step for Sri Lankan cricket. By 1981 the country had been awarded full Test status.

A raised level of expectation did not rest well on their shoulders when Sri Lanka returned to England for the 1983 tournament. They lost their first four group matches before facing New Zealand for a second time at Derby, desperate to restore some pride. They restricted New Zealand to 181 and reached the target for the loss of seven wickets with 7.1 overs to spare. However, they were brought back down to Earth in the final group match, losing to England by nine wickets at Headingley.

Sri Lanka struggled in 1987, too. Placed in a tough group alongside

Right: Mahela Jayawardene was a standout performer for Sri Lanka when they reached the ICC Cricket World Cup final in both 2007 and 2011.

England, Pakistan and the Windies, they did not win a single game and ended bottom of the group.

When the 1992 tournament's organizers announced that the first stage would be different, with all nine countries in one group, Sri Lanka were arguably the biggest beneficiaries. They would face another "lesser" cricketing light (Zimbabwe) with a realistic chance of achieving a victory that would not be considered a huge shock. They met in their opening match, in New Plymouth, New Zealand – and what a match it turned out to be. Zimbabwe batted first and posted an imposing 312 for 4 off their 50 overs; Arjuna Ranatunga (88 not out) led Sri Lanka's reply as they edged over the winning line for the loss of seven wickets with four balls to spare.

They lost their next match, to New Zealand, by six wickets, and their match against India was abandoned before they faced tournament newcomers South Africa in Wellington. Sri Lanka had a day to remember, bowling out South Africa for 195 and battled bravely with the bat to win by three wickets with one ball to spare. They lost their final four matches, but this had been their best *ICC* Cricket World Cup showing to date.

Still, no one was prepared for their performances at the 1996 tournament. They gained their first points of the campaign when they were awarded a victory after Australia decided not to travel to Colombo due to security concerns and then notched up a comfortable six-wicket

victory over Zimbabwe, before the Windies followed Australia's suit to hand Sri Lanka their third "victory" of the tournament. The first glimpse of Sri Lanka's true potential came in their fourth match, against India in Delhi. India batted first and posted an impressive 271 for 3, but Sri Lanka's response was as revealing as it was explosive. Their openers, Sanath Jayasuriya (79) and Romesh Kaluwitharana (26), seeking to take full advantage of the fielding restrictions in the first 15 overs, came out of the blocks firing. They raced to 50 off the first five overs and Sri Lanka reached the target for the loss of four wickets with eight balls to spare. They crushed Kenya by 144 runs in their final group

match and thumped England in the quarter-finals by five wickets in Faisalabad, with Jayasuriya smashing a 44-ball 82. They had their bowlers to thank in the semi-final against India in Calcutta. Sri Lanka batted first and posted 251 for 8; India slipped to 120 for 8 in reply when their fans, having seen enough, started to riot in the stands. The match was abandoned and Sri Lanka were awarded the win by default. Could Sri Lanka's bombastic approach succeed against streetwise Australia in the final? It seemed as though it would not when, chasing 242 for victory, they lost both openers with only 23 runs on the board. But this was far more than a one-dimensional Sri Lankan side. Aravinda de Silva hit an unbeaten 107 to guide Sri Lanka to an emphatic seven-wicket victory. Their success was welcomed around the cricket world.

They made a poor defence of their crown in 1999, though. They lost their opening two matches, against England and South Africa and, despite victories over Zimbabwe and Kenya, a

Above left: Muttiah Muralitharan took a Sri Lanka record 68 wickets at five ICC Cricket World Cups between 1996 and 2011.

Above right: Angelo Mathews has consistently shown himself to be Sri Lanka's leading batsman in recent times.

TEAM STATS

Captain: Dinesh Chandimal
Coach: Chandika Hathurusingha
Key players: Upul Tharanga, Angelo Mathews, Dinesh Chandimal, Lasith Malinga, Thisara Perera

Right: *Lasith Malinga adds pace and accuracy to the Sri Lankan bowling attack. There's possibly no finer death bowler in world cricket.*

In home conditions in 2011, Sri Lanka revelled, winning four of their six group matches (with one no result) to finish second in Group A. They thrashed England by ten wickets in the quarter-final in Colombo, then proved too strong for New Zealand in the last four, bowling them out for 217 and reaching the target with 2.1 overs to spare to reach the final – against India in Mumbai. They didn't do too much wrong in the final, either, with Mahela Jayawardene leading the way stroking a magnificent unbeaten 103 as Sri Lanka posted a challenging total of 274 for 6. But India rose to the challenge, reaching the target with ten balls to spare. They may have lost, but Sri Lanka had played a full part in the most high-quality final in *ICC* Cricket World Cup history.

They started well in Australia and New Zealand in 2015, winning four of their six group matches to progress comfortably through the group stages, but then crumbled in the quarter-finals. Batting first against South Africa in Sydney, they collapsed to 133 all out and South Africa chased down the target in just 18 overs.

Sri Lanka have lost some major players since then. World-class stalwarts Mahela Jayawardene, Kumar Sangakkara and Tillakaratne Dilshan have all slipped into retirement and this is a side that is, quite naturally, struggling to fill the void that their departures have created. Upul Tharanga, Niroshan Dickwella and Angelo Mathews have all scored heavily with the bat in recent times, and Lasith Malinga and off-spinner Akila Dananjaya have both proved themselves to be impressive performers with the ball, but the 2019 *ICC* Cricket World Cup might come just too early for this Sri Lanka side. They will expect to reach the quarter-finals, but anything beyond that would be a major achievement.

further defeat to India saw them fail to progress to the Super Sixes. Sri Lanka returned to form in 2003, however, topping their group with four wins and a tie from their six matches and then winning their final match in the Super Six stage to qualify for the semi-finals. They were no match for Australia, despite restricting them to 212 for 7, as they could not master either the pitch or Australia's bowlers and a rain-revised target was well beyond them.

They revelled in the conditions in the Caribbean in 2007, too, and finished top of their group with three wins out of three. In the Super Eights, four victories saw them finish second in the table to earn a semi-final place against New Zealand in Kingston, Jamaica. They had captain Mahela Jayawardene (115 not out) to thank as they posted 289 for 5, before Muttiah Muralitharan (4 for 31) spun them to an emphatic 81-run victory. Australia were too strong in the final, though. Batting first, Australia raced to 281 for 4 and Sri Lanka fell 51 runs short of a rain-reduced revised target (269).

AFGHANISTAN

Afghanistan's remarkable rise to the top table of world cricket has been one of the most heart-warming stories of recent years – and not only in sport. Back in 2010, then US Secretary of State Hillary Clinton was moved to say: "If we are hoping for a model of how to meet tough, international challenges with skill, dedication, and teamwork, we need only look to the Afghan national cricket team."

ALTHOUGH THERE IS EVIDENCE of British troops playing cricket in Kabul as far back 1839, the roots of the game in Afghanistan can be traced to northern Pakistan, and to the many refugee camps to where Afghans had fled in their thousands following the Soviet invasion of their country in the late 1970s and 1980s. It was here that children first developed a profound and lasting love for the game, playing among the makeshift tents with bats made of sticks, cardboard wickets and paper balls. In 1995, against the backdrop of turmoil in the region, the Afghanistan Cricket Board was first formed. When the war in Aghanistan finally came to an end, the refugees returned to their homeland, and took cricket with them. However, the ruling Taliban party banned all sport in the country, until 2000, when the ban on cricket – and only cricket – was lifted. The game had lift-off.

In 2001, Afghanistan became an Affiliate Member of the *ICC*; the same year, the newly-formed national team played in the second tier of Pakistan domestic cricket. While they were doing so, their country was plunged into fresh turmoil by the events that followed 9/11. But that did not stop them. By 2004, the team had started playing in Asian regional tournaments, finishing sixth in their first-ever appearance in the ACC trophy – a limited-overs tournament organized

Above left: Afghanistan's players celebrate victory over Scotland at the 2015 ICC Cricket World Cup.

Below: Afghanistan's all-time leading run-scorer in one-day international cricket with 4,471 runs, including six centuries, is Mohammad Shahzad.

TOURNAMENT STATS

World ranking: 10
Overall tournament record: P 6, W 1, L 5, Tied 0, No result 0
CWC best: Group stage (2015)
All-time leading batsman: Samiullah Shenwari (2015) – 254 runs
Best batting: 96 – Samiullah Shenwari v Scotland at Dunedin on 26 February 2015
All-time leading bowler: Shapoor Zadran (2015) – 10 wickets
Best bowling: 4 for 38 – Shapoor Zadran v Scotland at Dunedin on 26 February 2015

by the Asian Cricket Council for Associate and Affiliate Members. In 2006, they were runners-up behind Bahrain in the Middle East Cup. They toured England that year, too, playing mostly against County Second XIs, winning six of their seven matches.

The improvement was there for all to see: they finished third in that year's ACC Trophy, behind Hong Kong and the United Arab Emirates. The following year they collected their first trophy: the ACC Twenty20 trophy – shared with Oman after the final between the two sides ended in a tie. In 2008, Afghanistan won Division Five of the World Cricket League (held in Jersey); and, later that year, in Tanzania, won Division Four too. They were marching through the ranks: they won Division Three in 2009 and, although Afghanistan failed to qualify for the 2011 *ICC* Cricket World Cup, they did earn one-day international status for the next four years. It was a significant moment.

Afghanistan played their first-ever one-day international match against Scotland in Benoni, South Africa, on 19 April 2009. And they got off to a fantastic start: batting first, they posted 295 for 8 (Mohammad Nabi top-scoring with 58) and then bowled out Scotland for 206 to win by 89 runs. They went on to win the ACC Twenty20 Cup later in the year.

The next significant stage in their development came when they played in the *ICC* Intercontinental Cup – a series of matches played between 2011 and 2013 that effectively served

as a qualifying tournament for the 2015 *ICC* Cricket World Cup. They finished second in the group table, behind Ireland, to gain one of the four qualification spots.

There were more significant moments before that tournament, too. In 2013, they became an Associate Member of the *ICC*, which meant better exposure and, crucially, more funding for Afghanistan's players. In 2014, while preparing for the 2015 *ICC* Cricket World Cup, they recorded notable ODI victories over Bangladesh (by 32 runs in Fatullah) and Zimbabwe (twice). And then came the tournament itself.

Right: Captain Asghar Afghan has played more than 150 one-day internationals for Afghanistan since he made his debut in 2009.

Afghanistan's first match at the game's biggest tournament came against Bangladesh at Canberra. Bangladesh batted first and posted 267 all out; Afghanistan slipped to 3 for 3 in reply and never recovered: Samiullah Shenwari (42) and captain Mohammad Nabi (44) added a gloss of respectability to their total, but Afghanistan slipped to 162 all out to lose by 105 runs. They fared slightly better with the bat in their second game, against Sri Lanka in Dunedin, posting 232 (Asghar Afghan top-scoring with 54), and although Sri Lanka wobbled in their reply, losing both openers for golden ducks, Mahela Jayawardene struck a patient century (100) to help his side home with four wickets in hand and 1.4 overs to spare.

Next came fellow-qualifier Scotland – and an opportunity for Afghanistan to post a first-ever victory at the *ICC* Cricket World Cup. They produced their best performance of the tournament when it mattered: Shapoor Zadran (4 for 38) was the pick of the bowlers as Scotland slipped to 210 all out, while Samiullah Shenwari (96) shone with the bat. However, when he fell in the 47th over, to leave Afghanistan on 192 for 9, still 19 runs short of victory, Scotland must have sensed their opportunity. However, Afghanistan's last-wicket pair, Hamid Hassan (15 not out) and Shapoor Zadran (12 not out), held their nerve to see their side home with three balls to spare. It was a memorable victory. Although Afghanistan went on to suffer three heavy defeats in their

final three matches – against Australia (by 275 runs), against New Zealand (by six wickets) and against England (by nine wickets) – their 2015 *ICC* Cricket World Cup had been a positive experience for Afghanistan: they had proved that they belonged among the game's elite.

Could they maintain their upward momentum? In October 2015, they toured Zimbabwe and won the five-match one-day series 3–2: it was the first time in cricket history that a non-Test nation had beaten a Test nation in a series. In 2016, they gained enormous credit despite losing 3–2 to Bangladesh. They toured Zimbabwe again in January and February of 2017, again winning 3–2, and gained a creditable 1–1 series draw against the Windies in the Caribbean.

In March 2018, they travelled to Zimbabwe for the ten-team qualification tournament for the 2019 *ICC* Cricket World Cup and, initially at least, struggled. They lost their first three matches of the tournament – to Scotland (by seven wickets), Zimbabwe (by two runs) and Hong Kong (by 30 runs) – to leave their

Below: *Samiullah Shenwari was Afghanistan's leading run-scorer at the 2015 ICC Cricket World Cup, with 254 runs.*

TEAM STATS

Captain: Asghar Afghan
Coach: Phil Simmonds
Key players: Mohammad Shahzad, Asghar Afghan, Samiullah Shenwari, Rashid Khan, Shapoor Zadran

Above: Shapoor Zadran led the way with the ball for Afghanistan during the 2015 ICC Cricket World Cup, taking 10 wickets, including 4 for 38 against Scotland.

saw the whole of the cricket world stand up and take notice. They were outstanding. They beat Sri Lanka in their opening match (by 91 runs) and then thumped Bangladesh in their second (by 136 runs) to get off to a blistering start. Afghanistan then lost to Pakistan (by three wickets) and Bangladesh (by three runs), but produced a performance to remember against India in their final match of the campaign. Mohammad Shahzad hit a sparkling 116-ball 124 as Afghanistan posted 252 for 8; and India, mighty India, could only match their total in reply (252 all out). The match was tied: Afghanistan had come within a whisker of producing one of the biggest shocks in cricket history.

All of which will stand them in good stead when the 2019 *ICC* Cricket World Cup comes around. But Afghanistan's presence at this tournament will be about far more than simply results. It will be about celebrating a team that has surmounted obstacles unknown to most players – terrorism, displacement, and war – to rise from cricket obscurity to the big time. Every one of their players has a powerful backstory: such as all-rounder Samiullah Shenwari, who, as a baby spent weeks crossing the perilous mountains bordering Afghanistan and Pakistan to escape the invading Soviet army; or Mohammad Nabi whose father was kidnapped in 2013; or Shapoor Zadran, who was attacked by gunmen in 2017.

Afghanistan's exploits on the cricket pitch have won them admirers the world over. This is a team that has yet to play a match in its own country, but whose victories are celebrated wildly throughout the whole of Afghanistan. Let's hope that the 2019 *ICC* Cricket World Cup can give this side, and the country that it represents, at least one victory to remember.

hopes of qualification hanging by a thread. They did beat Nepal (by six wickets) in their final group match to give themselves an outside chance of progressing to the Super Sixes, but needed other results to go in their favour. The cricket gods shone on them: when Hong Kong lost their final group match to Nepal (by five wickets), Afghanistan secured the final spot in the group at their expense. They had made the Super Sixes by the skin of their teeth, but then produced a dramatic turnaround. They won all three of their matches to finish second in the Super Sixes table – securing 2019 *ICC* Cricket World Cup qualification by beating Ireland – and then went on to beat the Windies by seven wickets in the final. It was mission accomplished, but only just.

But then, in August 2018, came the Asia Cup in the United Arab Emirates – and Afghanistan's performances

WINDIES

WINDIES

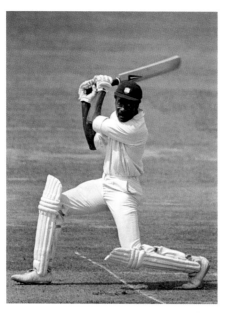

For anyone who saw the Windies when they were at the peak of their powers in the 1970s and 1980s, it is almost inconceivable to imagine that, some four decades later, they would only be appearing at the 2019 *ICC* Cricket World Cup by dint of securing the tournament's final qualifying spot – but that is a sign of just how far the stock of cricket has fallen in the Caribbean in recent years.

BUT LET'S START WITH the Windies when they were at the peak. They were the team everyone feared, with a battery of 90 mph-plus bowlers, that cricket has seen neither before nor since, and a collection of free-scoring, stroke-making batsmen that frequently destroyed an opponent's bowling attack. As such, they were the overwhelming favourites to lift the trophy at the inaugural edition of the *ICC* Cricket World Cup, in England in 1975 – and they duly lived up to their billing. They were almost untouchable. They thumped Sri Lanka by nine wickets in their opening match at Old Trafford, edged past Pakistan by one wicket at Edgbaston and then steam-rollered Australia by seven wickets in their final group game (at The Oval) to qualify for the semi-finals, against New Zealand at The Oval. Their bowlers gave them the upper hand, combining to dismiss New Zealand for 158 before their batsmen led them over the winning line. Clive Lloyd (102) was the star of the final, against Australia, leading his side to 291 for 8. Australia batted valiantly in reply, but

Above left: Clive Lloyd starred in the 1975 ICC Cricket World Cup final with a match-winning 102.

Below left: Alvin Kallicharran (left) and Michael Holding celebrate victory over England at the 1979 ICC Cricket World Cup final.

TOURNAMENT STATS

World ranking: 9
Overall tournament record: P 71, W 41, L 29, Tied 0, No result 1
CWC best: Champions (1975, 1979)
All-time leading batsman: Brian Lara (1992–2007) – 1,225 runs
Best batting: 215 – Chris Gayle v Zimbabwe at Canberra on 24 February 2015
All-time leading bowler: Courtney Walsh (1987–99) – 27 wickets
Best bowling: 7 for 51 – Winston Davis v Australia at Leeds on 11 June 1983

rarely threatened to reach the target and ultimately slipped to 274 all out. As expected, the Windies had become cricket's first world champions.

It was a familiar story in 1979, too. The Windies thumped India by nine wickets in their opening match at Edgbaston, surrendered their first-ever *ICC* Cricket World Cup point when their match against Sri Lanka was lost to the rain, but made sure they qualified for the semi-finals with a comfortable 32-run victory over New Zealand in their final group game. They faced Pakistan in the semi-finals at The Oval and, batting first, got off to a blistering start. Openers Gordon Greenidge (73) and Desmond Haynes (65) put on 132 for the opening wicket as the Windies posted a total of 293 for 6. Pakistan could not keep up with the required run-rate and eventually slipped to 250 all out. In the final, against England, Viv Richards (138 not out) and Collis King (86) were the stars

as they led their side to an imposing total of 286 for 9. England's openers Mike Brearley (64) and Geoff Boycott (57) put on 129 for the opening wicket, but took 38 overs to do so; it left England needing 158 from the final 22 overs and the task proved too much for them. They lost their last seven wickets for just 11 runs and the Windies were world champions once again.

And everyone expected another repeat performance in 1983. But the first sign that the Windies might not have everything their own way came in their very first match of the tournament, against India at Old Trafford. India batted first and posted 262 for 8; the Windies slipped to 228 all out in reply – and experienced their first-ever taste of *ICC* Cricket World Cup defeat. How would they respond? Emphatically – or so it seemed. They won their next five matches on the bounce to qualify for the semi-finals. They were too strong for Pakistan at The Oval, restricting them to 184 for 8 and reaching the target for the loss of just two wickets to reach their third successive *ICC* Cricket World Cup final – to play India. Surely lightning could not strike twice. It seemed not when the Windies' bowlers combined to dismiss India for 183. But then the unimaginable happened: the Windies batsmen struggled, slipped to 140 all out and India, against all the odds, became world champions. The Windies' cloak of invincibility had finally slipped – and this match, more than any other in recent times, proved to be a turning point in cricket history.

Below: Brian Lara is the Windies' all-time leading run-scorer at the ICC Cricket World Cup with 1,225 runs.

TEAM STATS

Captain: Jason Holder
Coach: Stuart Law
Key players: Shai Hope, Jason Holder,
Ashley Nurse, Kemar Roach,
Shannon Gabriel

The Windies' dominance was over.

Most commentators thought that the slower, lower pitches of the subcontinent would negate the Windies bowling firepower at the 1987 tournament – and so it proved. They did win three matches, but lost twice to England and, crucially, once to Pakistan to finish third in their group (behind England and Pakistan) and failed to qualify for the tournament's knockout stages.

They produced a similarly mixed bag of results in Australia and New Zealand in 1992, too. But thumping victories (such as a ten-wicket walloping of eventual champions Pakistan) were followed by disappointing defeats (such as a six-wicket loss to England after they were bowled out for 157) and their overall record of played eight, won four, lost four was not enough to see them qualify for the semi-finals.

A sign of just how far Windies cricket had fallen came when they crashed to 93 all out and a 73-run defeat to Kenya at the 1996 *ICC* Cricket World Cup in the subcontinent, but two wins, against Zimbabwe (by six wickets) and Australia (by four wickets) were enough to secure them the final qualifying spot in their group and a place in the quarter-finals. Brian Lara smashed an imperious 94-ball 111 as the Windies posted 264 for 8 in Karachi and then veteran off-spinner Roger Harper took 4 for 47 as South Africa slipped to 245 all out. Somewhat miraculously, the Windies had reached the semi-finals – and they very nearly made it to the final

as well. It is difficult to see how the Windies contrived to lose their semi-final match against Australia at Chandigarh. Their bowlers had reduced Australia to 15 for 4, before Stuart Law (72) and Michael Bevan (69) led the recovery to 207 for 8. When batting, the Windies reached 165 for 2, and seemed set for victory, only to lose their last eight wickets for 37 runs to lose by a paltry five runs.

And they have not come close to reaching the final since. In 1999, they won three and lost two of their group matches to miss out on a place in the Super Sixes. They repeated that performance in South Africa in 2003. All of which meant that the pressure

Below: Captain Jason Holder has proved himself to be a handy performer with both bat and ball.

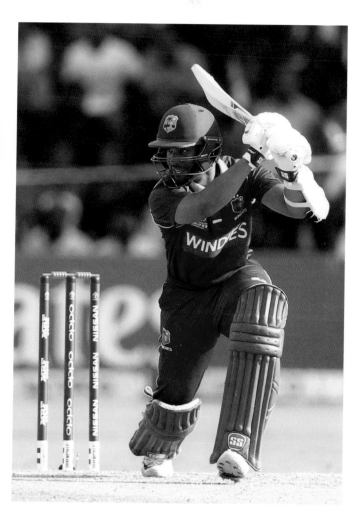

Above: *Shai Hope is the best of an emerging generation of Windies batsmen.*

Dhaka. Batting first, they slumped to a miserable 112 all out and Pakistan raced to victory without losing a wicket with a whopping 29.1 overs to spare. They scraped through the group stage in Australia and New Zealand in 2015, too (by dint of a superior tournament run-rate to Ireland), but then ran into New Zealand in the quarter-finals. Batting first, New Zealand posted a mammoth 393 for 6; in reply, the Windies were bowled out for 250 to lose by 143 runs.

And things have not got much better for the Windies since. Along with nine other teams, including Afghanistan, Ireland and Hong Kong, they were forced to travel to Zimbabwe in March 2018 in an attempt to win one of the two available qualification spots for the 2019 *ICC* Cricket World Cup and only got there by the skin of their teeth. And they have suffered some demoralizing and, considering their rich cricket history, ignominious defeats in recent times, including three losses to Afghanistan and a 2–1 home series defeat to Bangladesh. The talent is there. In 24-year-old batsman Shai Hope, they have a batsman of enormous potential; all-rounder and captain Jason Holder has proved that he can compete with the very best; in fast bowlers Kemar Roach and Shannon Gabriel they have two fast bowlers who evoke (albeit faint) memories of former West Indian fast-bowling glory. But this is a young, inexperienced and raw Windies side – and one that has suffered as a result of an indifferent selection policy that sees some of the region's best players plying their trade with huge success in the world's various Twenty20 leagues but not turning out for their country. Every lover of the game should be rooting for the Windies at the 2019 *ICC* Cricket World Cup: the global game desperately needs a competitive side from the Windies.

was well and truly on them when they hosted the tournament in 2007. They got off to a great start, beating Pakistan by 54 runs in their opening match at Kingston, Jamaica, and then recorded wins over Zimbabwe (by six wickets) and Ireland (by eight wickets) to finish top of their group and qualify for the Super Eights. But that is where the good news ended: somewhat ignominiously, they went on to lose five or their next six matches to crash out of their own tournament.

In 2011, they beat the Netherlands, Bangladesh and Ireland in the group stages to qualify for the quarter-finals (in fourth place in the group), but were then drubbed by Pakistan in

5 MAGIC MOMENTS:
Semi-final madness

South Africa have suffered some devastating moments of misfortune at the *ICC* Cricket World Cup, but some of those moments have been entirely of their own making. Take their *ICC* Cricket World Cup 1999 semi-final against Australia. South Africa dismissed Australia for an under-par 213 and then stuttered to 61 for 4 in reply. Lance Klusener's heroics left his side needing nine runs off the final over (with one wicket left), the chance of victory was still in their hands. Klusener smashed two fours from the first two balls, and the scores were level. The third ball: no run. The fourth ball: Klusener struck the ball to mid-off and set off for the run; his partner, Allan Donald, stayed where he was; both batsmen ended up at the bowler's end; and Donald was run out. Australia, who could barely believe their luck, had advanced to the final, and South Africa were left to rue their misfortune.

Opposite: Neither side can quite believe what has just happened as Allan Donald is run out to consign South Africa to defeat.

ICC CRICKET WORLD CUP STAR PLAYERS

Cricket is ultimately a team sport, but it is one in which individual quality can shine. Each side in the tournament is blessed with players of abundant quality, but if you're looking for the tournament's potential standout performers, then don't be too surprised if the players highlighted on the following pages feature heavily in the tournament's headlines. If these players perform to their full potential, their teams will come very close to lifting the trophy.

Opposite: *Virat Kohli will be aiming to win his second ICC Cricket World Cup with India, but this time as his nation's captain.*

SHAKIB
AL HASAN

Below: If Bangladesh are to cause an upset in 2019, Shakib Al Hasan will be pivotal.

Throughout Bangladesh's many on-pitch travails in recent years, Shakib Al Hasan has stood tall. So much so that many hardened observers of the game consider him to be the best cricketer his country has ever produced.

A TALENTED STROKEMAKER with the bat and an accurate, canny performer with the ball, coupled with an off-field professionalism that rivals that of the game's most dedicated players, make him the perfect benchmark for his fellow countrymen.

The left-hander made his debut, aged 19, against Zimbabwe in Harare in August 2006, scoring an unbeaten 30 to guide Bangladesh to an eight-wicket victory. His first century came in his second World Cup match, 134 not out against Canada at St John's, Antigua, at the 2007 tournament. And other impressive innings include: a 120-ball 108 against Pakistan in Multan in April 2008; an unbeaten 92 in a surprise five-wicket win over Sri Lanka at Dhaka in January 2009; and 106 in a nine-run defeat of New Zealand at Dhaka in October 2010. He has also made many vital contributions with the ball with a best of 5 for 47 against Zimbabwe at Dhaka in 2015. He's Bangladesh's only player to score more than 2,000 ODI runs (including a record seven 100s) and take more than 100 ODI wickets. Bangladesh victories against world cricket's big guns can be rare, but when they do happen, Shakib Al Hasan has usually been to the fore.

STATISTICS

Born: 24 March 1987, Magura, Jessore, Bangladesh
Debut: v Zimbabwe at Harare on 6 August 2006
Role: Left-hand bat; slow left-arm bowler
Matches: 191
Runs: 5,482
Centuries: 7
Average: 35.4
Highest score: 134 not out (v Canada at St John's, Antigua, on 25 February 2007)
Wickets: 243
Average: 29.57
Economy rate: 4.45
Best bowling: 5 for 47 (v Zimbabwe at Dhaka on 7 November 2015)

JASPRIT
BUMRAH

Below: Bumrah's unmistakable bowling action is as unusual as it is effective.

If you are looking for a player to define modern-age cricket, look no further than Jasprit Bumrah. His journey to the top of the game has been a difficult one, and were it not for T20 (a format in which he refined his game), he might not have made it all.

BY THE END OF 2014, Bumrah, a deceptively fast bowler with an unconventional action, had established himself as a regular member of the India A side, and promotion to the Test side beckoned. But then injury struck (to his left knee), he was sidelined for four months, and all the progress he had made came to a shuddering halt. However, a string of impressive performances in the Ranji Trophy, followed by some eye-catching bowling spells for the Mumbai Indians in the IPL, saw him called up to replace the injured Mohammed Shami for India's 2015–16 tour to Australia. Once there, he took his chance. He was India's leading wicket-taker during the 3–0 victory in the T20 series, and made his ODI debut on the same tour. He showed his real value to the Indian side during their 5–0 ODI series whitewash over Sri Lanka in 2017, where he took 15 wickets – including a career-best 5 for 27 in the third ODI in Pallekele – and was voted Player of the Series. He impressed during India's Test tour to England in 2018, too, and every Indian fan will be hoping for more of the same in 2019.

STATISTICS

Born: 6 December 1993, Ahmedabad, India
Role: Right-arm fast bowler
Debut: v Australia at Sydney on 23 January 2016
Matches: 37
Wickets: 64
Four wickets in an innings: 3
Five wickets in an innings: 1
Economy rate: 4.64
Strike rate: 29.0
Best bowling: 5 for 27 (v Sri Lanka at Pallekele on 27 August 2017)

HASAN
ALI

Below: *Few bowlers can claim better form in one-day cricket than Hasan Ali heading into the ICC Cricket World Cup in 2019.*

For those who grew up admiring Pakistan's fearsome pace duo Wasim Akram and Waqar Younis, Hasan Ali, at first glance, is a total opposite. He is in the new breed of fast bowler, full of variation and changes of pace, skills forged in the cricket's shorter formats to counter modern-day batsmen's all-out attack.

HE MADE HIS FIRST-CLASS debut at the tender age of 19, but put himself on the radar during Pakistan's domestic Twenty20 competition in 2015. He shone under the watchful eye of former Pakistan captain Shoaib Malik, picking up eight wickets in four matches. The following year, he took an impressive 17 wickets at 17.05 in Pakistan's domestic 50-over competition – and a call-up to the national XI duly followed. It proved a seamless transition from the domestic game to international cricket for Hasan Ali. He took four wickets against England in only his fifth game (at Cardiff on 4 September 2016); took 5 for 52 against Australia at Sydney four months later; 5 for 38 against the Windies at Providence on 9 April 2017; and a career-best 5 for 34 against Sri Lanka in Abu Dhabi on 18 October 2017. In fact, such has been his impact that since January 2017 only two bowlers in world cricket – Afghanistan's Rashid Khan (88) and England's Adil Rashid (62) – have taken more than his 59 one-day wickets.

STATISTICS

Born: 2 July 1994, Mandi Bahuddin, Punjab, Pakistan
Role: Right-arm medium-fast bowler
Debut: v Ireland at Dublin on 18 August 2016
Matches: 35
Wickets: 70
Four wickets in an innings: 1
Five wickets in an innings: 3
Economy rate: 5.19
Strike rate: 24.2
Best bowling: 5 for 34 (v Sri Lanka at Abu Dhabi on 18 October 2017)

RASHID
KHAN

Below: Already a star in the making, Rashid Khan is poised for a breakout tournament.

Quiz question: who has taken the most one-day international wickets since the start of 2017? Answer, incredibly: Afghanistan's Rashid Khan, who has taken 88 wickets in 34 matches (his nearest rival, England's Adil Rashid, has taken just 62 in comparison). But perhaps we should not be so surprised.

RASHID KHAN made his one-day international debut aged 17 against Zimbabwe in October 2015, and it did not take long before his quick-through-the-air, persistent combination of googlies and leg-spinners started to confound batsmen around the world. He took 4 for 21 against Ireland at Dublin in his 12th ODI, in July 2016; and 6 for 43 against the same opponent in India in March the following year. But he sent shockwaves around world cricket, taking 7 for 18 (off 8.4 overs) against the Windies at St Lucia, on 9 June 2017. The fourth-best bowling figures in one-day international cricket history, his performance helped Afghanistan to a shock 63-run victory. A star was born. The following year, his status as one of the game's global superstars was cemented when the Sunrisers Hyderabad paid US$1.4 million for his services for that year's IPL – making him his country's first IPL millionaire. A handy batsman with three ODI half-centuries and an athletic fielder, Rashid Khan may become one of the most talked-about players at *ICC Cricket World Cup 2019*.

STATISTICS

Born: 20 September 1998, Nangarhar, Afghanistan
Role: Right-arm leg-break and googly bowler
Debut: v Zimbabwe at Bulawayo on 18 October 2015
Matches: 52
Wickets: 118
Four wickets in an innings: 4
Five wickets in an innings: 4
Economy rate: 3.90
Strike rate: 22.2
Best bowling: 7 for 18 (v Windies at Gros Islet, St Lucia on 9 June 2017)

VIRAT
KOHLI

Below: Kohli's reputation as the biggest superstar in world cricket will be put to the test.

It's not too much of a stretch to say that Virat Kohli is the most influential figure in world cricket today and, across all formats of the game, its best player. He has achieved almost the impossible by stepping into Sachin Tendulkar's shoes, and every time he goes out to bat a billion diehard Indian fans expect greatness.

AND HE HAS NOT DISAPPOINTED: since the start of 2017 he has scored more runs than any other player in both ODI cricket (2,209 runs at an average of 88.36, with nine centuries) and Test cricket (1,938 runs at an average of 64.60, with eight centuries).

Kohli captained India to success at the *ICC Under-19 World Cup* in 2008. He then excelled for the Royal Challengers Bangalore in the IPL – after which sponsors rushed to his doorstep and made him a global star before he had even established himself in the India side. That did not take too long: his fearless approach to batting soon saw him become one of the most admired players in world cricket, and he cemented that perception when he played a pivotal role in India's march to the *ICC Cricket World Cup* crown in 2011. But it is as India's captain that he has garnered the most admirers. He has transferred his intense passion and work ethic onto the Indian side, helping them become one of the most complete teams in world cricket. All the while, he has continued to churn out the runs, hitting three consecutive 100s against the Windies in October 2018.

STATISTICS

Born: 5 November 1988, Delhi, India
Debut: v Sri Lanka at Dambullah on 18 August 2008
Role: Right-hand bat
Matches: 211
Runs: 9,779
Centuries: 35
Half-centuries: 48
Average: 58.20
Strike rate: 92.12
Highest score: 183 (v Pakistan at Dhaka on 18 March 2012)

SOUTH AFRICA CRICKET

KAGISO
RABADA

Below: *The task of leading South Africa's bowling corps will fall on Rabada's shoulders.*

The best fast bowler South Africa has produced in recent years, Kagiso Rabada burst onto the scene at the 2014 *ICC* Under-19 World Cup when he took 6 for 25 against Australia in the semi-final, helped South Africa to their first title, and ended the tournament as the leading wicket-taker.

BY THE END OF 2015, he had represented the senior South Africa side in all three formats of the game. His ODI career got off to a blistering start when, on his debut, against Bangladesh at Dhaka on 10 July 2015, he took 6 for 16 – his first three wickets coming in a hat-trick. They were the best figures ever recorded by a debutant in a one-day international and remain his career-best figures in an ODI to date.

It was a hard act to live up to, but Rabada has continued to cause problems to the world's best batsmen: he took 4 for 41 against India in Mumbai in October 2015, a match South Africa won by the staggering margin of 214 runs; he impressed with 4 for 45 as South Africa beat England by the slenderest of margins (one run) at Johannesburg in February 2016; and, more recently, in July 2018, was the pick of South Africa's bowlers (taking 4 for 41) as they recorded a rare five-wicket victory over Sri Lanka in Dambullah. Now the spearhead of an inexperienced South Africa attack, if the Proteas are to end their wait for an *ICC* Cricket World Cup victory, much will depend on the performances of Kagiso Rabada.

STATISTICS

Born: 25 May 1995, Johannesburg, South Africa
Debut: v Bangladesh at Dhaka on 10 July 2015
Role: Right-arm fast bowler
Matches: 52
Wickets: 81
Four wickets in an innings: 5
Five wickets in an innings: 1
Economy rate: 5.09
Strike rate: 32.5
Best bowling: 6 for 16 (v Bangladesh at Dhaka on 10 July 2015)

JOE
ROOT

Below: The batting skill of Joe Root represents England's best chance for a World Cup victory on home soil.

For all the headline-grabbing performances of Jos Buttler, Jonny Bairstow, Ben Stokes and others in the much-improved England team in recent years, Joe Root has been his side's most consistent performer – and its best batsman.

SINCE THE START OF 2017, only India's Virat Kohli (2,209) has scored more one-day international runs than the Yorkshireman's 1,783 (at a hefty average of 66.03). Perhaps we've all come to expect too much from the best English batsman of this generation – and plenty of others, too.

Root made his debut, aged 22, against India in Rajkot in January 2013, but had to wait 25 matches before passing three figures for the first time, when he scored a 122-ball 107 against the Windies in Antigua on 5 March 2014. A first home one-day international century arrived at his home ground, Headingley (Leeds), six months later (against India). His first *ICC* Cricket World Cup century came in 2015 – 121, in a losing cause against Sri Lanka at Wellington. He has, however, struggled to turn half-centuries into hundreds: since January 2017, he has passed 50 on 16 occasions, but reached three figures only five times – though he recorded his first back-to-back centuries against India in 2018. All England fans hope his spectacular form will continue in England and Wales in 2019.

STATISTICS

Born: 30 December 1990, Sheffield, England
Role: Right-hand bat
Debut: v India at Rajkot, 11 January 2013
Matches: 116
Runs: 4,800
Centuries: 13
Half-centuries: 28
Average: 51.61
Strike rate: 86.83
Highest score: 133 not out (v Bangladesh at
The Oval on 1 June 2017)

CRICKET
AUSTRALIA

MITCHELL
STARC

Below: The outstanding player of the ICC Cricket World Cup 2015 will look to recapture his form in 2019.

Among Australia's justifiably hyped battery of fast bowlers, Mitchell Starc is the best and most feared. Tall and fast, he is a left-arm swing bowler with admirable control who, on his day, is capable of blowing opposition batting line-ups away.

HE SHOWCASED that to spectacular effect during *ICC* Cricket World Cup 2015, ending the tournament with 22 wickets to his name (at an average of 10.18) and collecting the Player of the Tournament award as Australia won the *ICC* Cricket World Cup for the first time since 2007.

Starc made his debut back in 2010, but spent much of the early part of his international career living in the shadow of another Australian left-arm fast bowler: Mitchell Johnson. But where Johnson had the pace, Starc had the control, and he soon started to impress in the 50-over game. He took 4 for 27 against Sri Lanka at Brisbane in November 2010 in only his second ODI match; took five wickets in an innings for the first time (of five) against Pakistan in Sharjah in August 2012. A month before *ICC* Cricket World Cup 2015, he took 6 for 43 against India at Melbourne and bettered that during the tournament with a career-best 6 for 28 against New Zealand in Auckland. He has made only 13 one-day international appearances since the start of 2017 as Australia juggled personnel in an attempt to find their best XI. If Starc is fit and firing at *ICC* Cricket World Cup 2019, then Australia could be the team to beat.

STATISTICS

Born: 30 January 1990, Sydney, Australia
Debut: v India at Visakhapatnam on 20 October 2010
Role: Left-arm fast bowler
Matches: 72
Wickets: 141
Four wickets in an innings: 9
Five wickets in an innings: 5
Economy rate: 4.93
Strike rate: 25.4
Best bowling: 6 for 28 (v New Zealand at Auckland on 28 February 2015)

UPUL
THARANGA

Although he has frustrated in the Test arena, Upul Tharanga's 50-over record measures favourably against the giants of Sri Lankan cricket: only four of them – Mahela Jayawardene, Tillakaratne Dilshan, Kumar Sangakkara and Sanath Jayasuriya – have scored more than his total of 15 centuries.

AN ELEGANT LEFT-HANDED opening batsman, he shone at the *ICC* Under-19 *ICC* Cricket World Cup in 2004 and made his ODI debut the following year – just eight months after his family home on Sri Lanka's west coast had been swept away in the devastating 2004 Asian tsunami. He made his first century (105 against Bangladesh in Colombo) in only his fifth innings, and went on to form potent opening partnerships with first Jayasuriya and then Dilshan (the latter pair batted together on 77 occasions and notched up 3,367 runs, with nine 100-plus partnerships). He contributed to Sri Lanka's march to the final of the *ICC* Cricket World Cup 2011, scoring two centuries, including an unbeaten 102 against England in the quarter-final. His career-best 174 not out came against India at Kingston, Jamaica, in a July 2013 tri-nations tournament. Thuranga has become a veteran presence in Sri Lanka's new generation of players, and if he finds his form in England in 2019, Sri Lanka can go deep into the tournament.

Above: Sri Lanka's veteran opening batsman will look to inspire his country as he did in 2011.

STATISTICS

Born: 2 February 1985, Balapitiya, Sri Lanka
Role: Left-hand bat
Debut: v Windies at Dambulla, 2 August 2005
Matches: 230
Runs: 6,936
Centuries: 15
Half-centuries: 37
Average: 34.33
Strike rate: 75.97
Highest score: 174 not out (v India, Kingston, Jamaica, 2 July 2013)

NEW ZEALAND
BLACKCAPS

KANE
WILLIAMSON

Still only 28 years of age, Kane Williamson is already a New Zealand great, and by the time he has finished his career he may well be regarded as the greatest batsman his country has ever produced.

THE RIGHT-HANDED BATSMAN forged his reputation in the Test arena with a century on his debut, a doughty 131 against India in Ahmedabad in November 2010, and soon established himself as New Zealand's leading light. Of all current Test players, only Steve Smith (61.37), Virat Kohli (53.92) and Joe Root (51.04) have higher career averages than Williamson's 50.35. He is rightly considered to be among Test cricket's Big Four. But he has also proved to be mightily effective in the one-day arena.

His ODI career got off to an inauspicious start with two-consecutive ducks (albeit on turning wickets in India), but he soon got into his stride, recording his first century (108 v Bangladesh in Dhaka) in only his fifth knock, in October 2010. He then played in four of New Zealand's eight matches at *ICC* Cricket World Cup 2011. Williamson's career-best unbeaten 145 came against South Africa in Kimberley in January 2013, and he made important contributions as the Black Caps surprised many by reaching the final of the *ICC* Cricket World Cup 2015. He has not scored a century in the world's biggest one-day tournament, but it would be no surprise if he changes that unwanted record in England and Wales in 2019.

Above: The Black Caps's star batsman shouldn't be underestimated.

STATISTICS

Born: 8 August 1990, Tauranga, New Zealand
Debut: v India at Dambullah, 10 August 2010
Matches: 127
Runs: 5,156
Centuries: 11
Half-centuries: 33
Average: 46.87
Strike rate: 83.22
Highest score: 145 not out (v South Africa at Kimberley on 22 January 2013)

6 MAGIC MOMENTS:
Magical McGrath

It seems entirely appropriate that the finest fast bowler of his (and perhaps any) generation, Australia's Glenn McGrath, should have produced the best bowling figures ever recorded in a match at the *ICC* Cricket World Cup. The moment came when mighty Australia, the defending champions, played against Namibia, competing at the tournament for the first time, at Potchefstroom in the group stages of the *ICC* Cricket World Cup 2003. What followed was the most one-sided match the tournament had seen. Australia won the toss, batted first, and posted an inevitably unassailable target of 302. Enter McGrath, who took the wicket of Jan-Berrie Burger with his fourth ball and then proceeded to scythe his way through the Namibian batting line-up. By the time he had finished his day's work, he had taken 7 for 15 off seven overs to help skittle Namibia for 45 (off 14 overs) to lead Australia to a 256-run victory.

Opposite: *Glenn McGrath looks thrilled as he takes yet another Namibian wicket on the way to an historic haul at the ICC Cricket World Cup 2003.*

ICC CRICKET WORLD CUP HISTORY

The *ICC Cricket World Cup* was contested for the first time in England in 1975, just four years after the first-ever one-day international had been played. It has grown spectacularly over the years to become the flagship event on the international cricket calendar. The 2019 contest in England and Wales will be the 12th edition of the tournament, and it has a lot to live up to if it is to match the thrills and spills of the 11 tournaments played to date.

Opposite: *Australia celebrate their historic fifth ICC Cricket World Cup victory, after triumphing over their Antipodean neighbours New Zealand to win the 2015 tournament.*

1975

The inaugural *ICC* Cricket World Cup, contested by eight teams in England in 1975, was barely recognizable from the tournament we know today. Players wore white, the matches were 60 overs per side, and nobody quite knew what to expect – including the players.

ENGLAND'S TOURNAMENT-OPENING VICTORY over India in Group A, by the healthy margin of 202 runs at Lord's on 7 June, was notable for seeing the tournament's first-ever century – England's Dennis Amiss with 137. New Zealand thumped East Africa by 181 runs in the second Group A match, with Glenn Turner scoring an unbeaten 171. England's comprehensive 80-run victory over New Zealand at Trent Bridge (Keith Fletcher with 131) secured their place in the semi-finals, leaving India and New Zealand to fight it out for the group's final other last-four slot. India fell to an under-par 230 all out, and New Zealand won with seven balls and four wickets to spare.

Group B was decided after two rounds of games. Australia beat Pakistan by 73 runs in their opening match, while the Windies began with a comfortable nine-wicket win over Sri Lanka. The best game of the tournament saw the Windies edge past Pakistan by one wicket to reach the semi-finals. It had been a remarkable escape for the pre-tournament favourites – the final two wickets put on 110 runs. By beating Sri Lanka Australia joined the Windies as semi-finalists, but lost to them in their last group game.

The first semi-final saw England face Australia in swing friendly conditions at Headingley. Australia won a crucial toss, put England into bat and scythed through the host's batting line-up, with Gary Gilmour taking 6 for 14 as England collapsed to 93 all out. Australia lost six wickets of their own in reply, but reached the target with 31.2 overs to spare. The second semi-final,

Windies against New Zealand at The Oval, was an equally one-sided affair. New Zealand batted first and were dismissed for 158; the Windies reached the target with 19.1 overs remaining.

The final itself turned out to be a cracking affair. The Windies batted first and, led by Clive Lloyd's magnificent 102, reached 291 for 8 off their 60 overs. Australia replied resiliently, but, hindered by four run outs, ultimately fell short by 17 runs. The Windies had become one-day cricket's first world champions.

Above: Clive Lloyd lifts the ICC Cricket World Cup trophy after the 1975 final.

1979

Following the success of the inaugural *ICC* Cricket World Cup, the 1979 edition once again featured eight teams competing at six venues across England.

SEVEN OF THE NATIONS who had competed in 1975 returned to stake their claim to the title of world champions, with newcomers Canada replacing East Africa after finishing as runners-up in the 1979 *ICC* Trophy to Sri Lanka. In what was a wide-open field, the Windies were understandably favoured as reigning champions, but New Zealand and Pakistan also entered the tournament in good form, while the hosts, England, were confident of a strong run on home soil.

The Windies opened their campaign with a comfortable nine-wicket victory over India, while New Zealand matched the result against Sri Lanka in the other Group A match. New Zealand then booked their place in the semi-finals when they eased to an eight-wicket victory over India,

while the Windies' match against Sri Lanka fell victim to the rain. India's miserable tournament came to an end when they lost to Sri Lanka by 47 runs at Old Trafford, before the Windies edged past New Zealand by 32 runs at Trent Bridge to book their place in the last four.

England won all of their matches to top Group B, which meant that the second semi-final place would go to the winner of the Pakistan-Australia clash at Trent Bridge: Pakistan won by 89 runs.

In the first semi-final at Old Trafford, Mike Brearley (53) and Graham Gooch (71) held the England innings together as the hosts reached 221 for 8. John Wright (69) did the same for New Zealand, but the Kiwis fell nine runs short. In the second semi-final at The Oval, the Windies (293 for 6) proved too strong for Pakistan, who reached 250 all out.

England initially took control of the final, reducing the Windies to 99 for 4, but then the Windies rallied and, led by Viv Richards (138 not out) and Collis King (86) reached an imposing 286 for 9. England's reply never got going. Their 129-run opening partnership between Brearley (64) and Geoff Boycott (57) was solid but terminally slow and as the run-rate spiralled wickets fell. Joel Garner (5 for 38) was almost unplayable as England lost their last six wickets for 11 runs to be 194 all out and the Windies tasted *ICC* Cricket World Cup glory once more.

Above: *Hundreds of Windies fans invade the pitch at Lord's to celebrate their side's victory.*

1983

The *ICC* Cricket World Cup 1983 saw a few tweaks to the format: each team played the others in the group twice and a fielding circle was introduced, but the main question in the build-up was if anyone could unseat the defending champions, the Windies.

COULD IT BE ENGLAND, with star all-rounder Ian Botham in his prime? Or could Pakistan produce the maverick performance everyone knew they were capable of when it really mattered? One thing was for certain: few experts fancied India's chances.

England and Pakistan both showed their hands in the opening round of matches in Group A, England beating New Zealand by 106 runs at The Oval, while Pakistan cruised to a 50-run victory against Sri Lanka. However, when New Zealand thumped Pakistan by 52 runs at Edgbaston, it

Above: Kapil Dev holding the World Cup after India beat the Windies in the ICC Cricket World Cup 1983 final.

became a three-horse race for the group's two semi-final spots. England secured one of them, which meant that the final Group A match, the second between Pakistan and New Zealand was critical. Pakistan had to score enough runs to boost their run-rate and win: they posted 261 for 3 off their 60 overs and won by 11 runs to satisfy both requirements.

The first major shock of the tournament came in the opening round of matches in Group B when India beat the Windies by 34 runs at Old Trafford. The Windies recovered to win the remainder of their group matches to claim the first semi-final spot, while India traded wins with Australia (critically by 118 runs in their second encounter) to claim the other.

In the first semi-final at Old Trafford, India restricted England to 213 and cantered to the target with six wickets and 3.5 overs to spare. In the second semi-final at The Oval, the Windies' bowlers stifled Pakistan (184 for 8) before their batsmen blew them away, easing to the target in the 49th over for the loss of two wickets.

Still, nobody fancied India to upset the Windies in the final – particularly when they slipped to 183 all out batting first. Then the magic occurred. India's star all-rounder, Kapil Dev, had famously uttered that it might not have been a "winning total", but it "was a fighting one". And so it proved: India's bowlers exploited both the weather and the pitch to perfection to dismiss a shell-shocked Windies for 140 to complete one of the most remarkable upsets in cricket history.

1987

The tournament moved from England to the subcontinent (with India and Pakistan as co-hosts). It was the first to be played as 50 overs per side games and to feature neutral umpires.

IT WAS ALSO A TOURNAMENT that refused to follow the script: an India–Pakistan final seemed to be on the cards as the tournament progressed. Things, however, did not turn out that way.

Geoff Marsh (110) was the hero for Australia as they beat India by one run in their opening Group A match, and although Australia lost the return match in Delhi (by 56 runs), they won all of their other matches to progress to the semi-finals. India's Delhi win was also enough to see them into the last four.

Pakistan started their Group B campaign with a nervy 15-run win over Sri Lanka at Hyderabad. In the group's other opening-round match, England scraped to a two-wicket victory over the Windies. It turned out to be a crucial victory for England, because, although they went on to lose to Pakistan, a comfortable 108-run victory over Sri Lanka was enough to see them through to the semi-finals. England's progress meant that the Windies, having lost by one run to Pakistan in their first meeting, were eliminated, even though they did record a 28-run victory in their final group match. It marked the beginning of the end for the great Windies side of the 1970–80s.

The first semi-final saw Pakistan play Australia in Lahore. Before the match, Pakistan batsman Zaheer Abbas had dubbed the Australians a "bunch of club cricketers". His words provided the Aussies with an extra incentive: they reached 267 for 8 off their 50 overs before dismissing Pakistan for 249 to reach the final.

Graham Gooch (115) and Mike Gatting (56) were the heroes for England against India in the second semi-final in Mumbai. The pair swept England to a challenging 254 for 6 before India collapsed to 219 all out.

The final was a captivating affair. Australia batted first and posted 253 for 5. In reply, England seemed to be cruising towards the target, reaching 135 for 2, before Gatting, inexplicably, reverse swept Allan Border's first ball into the hands of wicketkeeper Greg Dyer to fall for 41. England never recovered and eventually fell eight runs short of victory to hand Australia their first ICC Cricket World Cup victory.

Above: *Allan Border with the World Cup trophy following the 1987 final.*

1992

Australia and New Zealand hosted the first *ICC* Cricket World Cup to include all Test-playing nations (South Africa made their tournament debut after 21 years of cricket isolation). It was also the first to see players in coloured clothing, using white balls and playing under floodlights.

IT ALSO TURNED OUT to be a spectacular last hurrah for Pakistan's great all-rounder Imran Khan, who led his side to a memorable victory.

The tournament's revised format saw each team playing the other to decide the four semi-finalists. It started in dramatic fashion when New Zealand beat pre-tournament favourites, defending champions Australia, in the opening game by 37 runs in Auckland. The rollercoaster ride continued. England beat India in Perth; the Windies seemed to have rediscovered their mojo when they beat Pakistan by 10 wickets in Melbourne; Australia's unexpected slump continued when they lost to South Africa by nine wickets in Sydney. And by the time the 36 group matches had been completed, the four teams left standing were: New Zealand (who had won all but one of their eight matches), England, South Africa and Pakistan (whose final group-game victory over New Zealand edged them into the last four – at Australia's expense).

New Zealand faced Pakistan in the first semi-final in Auckland. Their star batsman, Martin Crowe, was nursing a troublesome hamstring and faced the stark choice of either playing and aggravating it or resting it for the final (should New Zealand get there). He opted for the latter, and watched on in dismay as Pakistan, led by Inzamam-ul-Haq's 60, chased down their target of 263 with one over to spare.

The second semi-final between England and South Africa in Sydney is remembered for all the wrong reasons. England had batted first in a rain-reduced match and reached 252 for 6 off 45 overs. South Africa had reached 232 for 6 off 42.5 overs in reply when the rain started once more: when the rain finally stopped, the much-criticized rain rule stated they needed an impossible 23 runs off one ball. England had scraped through to the final and South Africa were incredulous.

But if England rode their luck in the semi-final, they were overpowered by Pakistan in the final. A limited-overs record crowd of 87,812 watched on as Pakistan posted a target of 250 and then blew England away for 227 to provide their captain, Imran Khan, with the perfect send-off.

Above: *Wasim Akram (Pakistan) bowls Chris Lewis (England) in the final of the ICC Cricket World Cup 1992.*

1996

CHAMPIONS: SRI LANKA
TEAMS: 12
HOSTS: INDIA, PAKISTAN
AND SRI LANKA

The *ICC* Cricket World Cup returned to the subcontinent in 1996, but with a change of format: 12 teams were invited to take part, meaning that Kenya, the Netherlands, and the United Arab Emirates made their first *ICC* Cricket World Cup appearances.

THE TEAMS WERE SPLIT into two groups of six, with the top four in each group advancing to the knockout phase.

Sri Lanka's campaign started in bizarre fashion when they "won" their opening Group A match against Australia in Colombo by walkover – the Australians, concerned by security problems in Colombo, simply stayed in Mumbai and forfeited the match. The Windies then did the same, so the first sight we got of Sri Lanka came when they played India in Delhi. Sachin Tendulkar scored a majestic 137 to lead India to an imposing 271 for

Above: *Aravinda de Silva (Sri Lanka) celebrates reaching his century in the final of the ICC Cricket World Cup 1996 against Australia.*

3, before Sanath Jayasuriya thrashed his way to 79 to lead Sri Lanka to the target with six wickets and eight balls to spare. Both Sri Lanka and India advanced to the knockout stages, where they were joined by Australia and the Windies (who overcame a shock defeat to Kenya).

Group B was a more orderly, and predictable, affair, with South Africa topping the group followed by Pakistan, New Zealand and England.

The tournament really came alive in the knockout stages: Jayasuriya smashed a 44-ball 82 to lead Sri Lanka to a comfortable five-wicket victory over England; India were too strong for Pakistan in Lahore; the Windies beat South Africa in Karachi; and Australia edged past New Zealand in Chennai.

Sri Lanka recovered from 35 for 3 to post 251 for 8 against India in the first semi-final in Calcutta and won by default when the home crowd rioted after India had slumped to 120 for 8 in reply. In the second semi-final in Chandigarh, the Windies seemed set for victory, chasing 208 against Australia, only to lose their nerve as they lost their last seven wickets for 37 runs.

And so Sri Lanka and Australia finally got to play each other – in the final in Lahore. Australia, batting first, posted a competitive 241 for 7. In reply, Aravinda de Silva scored a magnificent unbeaten century (107) to lead his side to a comfortable seven-wicket victory with 20 balls to spare. Sri Lanka's victory – a triumph for a comparative cricketing underdog – was welcomed around the world.

1999

CHAMPIONS: AUSTRALIA
TEAMS: 12
HOSTS: ENGLAND, IRELAND, THE NETHERLANDS, SCOTLAND AND WALES

The 1999 edition of the event again had 12 teams split into two groups of six, but this time only the top three advanced to a Super Six stage. Here, each team played the three which had advanced from the other group, but retained the points they had won in the first stage. If this sounds complicated, it was.

THE FIRST HALF OF THE TOURNAMENT was all about England's travails. For the organizers, the worst-case scenario was that England would suffer an early departure from the event. Despite thumping defeats of Sri Lanka and Kenya in their opening two games, the bad dream became reality as they lost heavily to South Africa, beat Zimbabwe, and went into their final group game needing to beat India and hoping South Africa defeated Zimbabwe. Zimbabwe won by 48 runs, England lost by 63 runs and exited the 37-day tournament on day 16. South Africa, India and Zimbabwe advanced from Group A.

Pakistan were best in Group B and were joined in the Super Sixes by Australia and New Zealand.

In the Super Sixes, no team was able to assert any real authority over the others. The upshot was that Pakistan, Australia and South Africa advanced to the last four with records of played five won three, while New Zealand edged past Zimbabwe on net run-rate.

Pakistan were at their magnificent best against New Zealand at Old Trafford. Bowling first, they restricted New Zealand to 241 for 7 before Saeed Anwar (113 not out) and Wajahatullah Wasti (84) led them to a comfortable nine-wicket victory. The second semi-final between Australia and South Africa at Edgbaston will linger long in the memory. South Africa, chasing 213, reached 212 for 9, with four balls remaining. Allan Donald was run out in farcical manner with three balls left to leave the game tied. Thanks to Australia's better tournament net run-rate against South Africa, they reached the final.

All the drama, however, was used up in the semi-finals and the final proved to be a disappointing, anti-climactic affair. Pakistan, batting first, imploded and crashed to 132 all out. Australia then powered their way to victory with eight wickets in hand and 29.5 overs to spare.

Above: Shane Warne (Australia) celebrates bowling Ijaz Ahmed (Pakistan) in the final of the ICC Cricket World Cup 1999 at Lord's.

2003

The 2003 tournament was totally dominated by an Australia team packed with highly skilled individuals, especially Glenn McGrath with the ball and captain Ricky Ponting with the bat. The absence of the banned Shane Warne was barely noticed and they produced a string of spectacular performances.

THE ONLY DOWNSIDE was that England's refusal to travel to Zimbabwe and New Zealand's similar decision to stay away from Kenya (with the points being awarded to their opponents), gave the back-end of the tournament a somewhat skewed look. Australia, India and Zimbabwe advanced from Group A, while Sri Lanka, Kenya and New Zealand went forward from Group B. By the time the Super Sixes had been completed, the four teams in the semi-finals were Australia, India, Sri Lanka and Kenya.

Australia were proving to be the tournament's class act. The defending champions had been supreme, winning all of their matches, and only being troubled once: against England on a slow, low wicket at Port Elizabeth – the venue for their semi-final clash against Sri Lanka.

In the last four game, again stifled by the pitch, Australia limped to 212 for 7 off their 50 overs, thanks for the most part to an uncharacteristically patient innings of 91 from Andrew Symonds, but Sri Lanka never threatened to reach their rain-reduced target (172 off 38.1 overs), falling 49 runs short. In the second semi-final in Durban, India proved too strong for Kenya, reaching 270 for 4 (with captain Sourav Ganguly hitting a fine unbeaten 111) before dismissing the Kenyans for 179 (Zaheer Khan the pick of the bowlers with 3 for 14).

And so the tournament's two best teams had made it through to the final in Johannesburg – and Australia prevailed. Batting first, they raced to 359 for 2, thanks to captain Ricky Ponting's magnificent 140 off 121 balls. India never recovered after losing Sachin Tendulkar to the fifth ball of their reply, and slipped to 234 all out in the 39th over. Australia had become the first team to make a successful *ICC* Cricket World Cup defence since the Windies in 1979.

Above: *Ricky Ponting racks up the runs against India in the ICC Cricket World Cup 2003 final. The Australian would finish with a total of 140.*

2007

An increase to 16 teams meant the tournament format was changed yet again. The teams were split into four groups of four, with the top two sides advancing to a Super Eight group, in which they would play all the other qualified teams apart from the team they had played in their group – those points were carried over.

AUSTRALIA AND SOUTH AFRICA qualified from Group A; Sri Lanka and Bangladesh (who both beat India) advanced from Group B; New Zealand and England emerged from Group C; while the Windies and Ireland (who had pulled off the shock of the tournament when they beat Pakistan) advanced from Group D.

Australia, having already beaten South Africa in the group stage, dominated the Super Eights, winning all six of their matches. They were joined in the semi-finals by Sri Lanka, South Africa and New Zealand.

Sri Lanka played New Zealand in the first semi-final, in Kingston, Jamaica. Batting first, they reached an imposing 289 for 5, Mahela Jayawardene top-scoring with an unbeaten 115. In reply, New Zealand could not cope with Sri Lanka's spin attack, particularly Muttiah Muralitharan (4 for 31) and slipped to 208 all out. The second semi-final at Gros Islet, St Lucia, between Australia and South Africa was even more one-sided. South Africa collapsed to 149 all out and Australia cantered to the target with 19.3 overs to spare.

The final was a repeat of the one in 1996, but with a different outcome. Adam Gilchrist (149) was the star of this final, helping Australia to a formidable 281 for 4 off 38 (rain-restricted) overs. Sri Lanka never threatened the target and ended on 215 for 8. Australia had completed an unprecedented hat-trick of tournament wins.

No one could deny Australia their moment. They had been the class act of the tournament: they scored 300-plus runs every time they had batted first (apart from in the rain-reduced final); never lost more than six wickets in an innings; and won by more than 200 runs on three occasions. Four Australia batsmen featured among the tournament's top-ten run-scorers and four bowlers were in the top-ten wicket-takers. The brutal truth for the other teams was that none of them could live with them. These Australians might be remembered as being the best one-day side in history, better than the great Windies from the 1970s and early 1980s.

Above: *Australia's talismanic Adam Gilchrist inspired his team to a victory that never really looked in doubt.*

2011

A reduction to 14 teams meant that the format for the *ICC* Cricket World Cup 2011 had to change yet again. This time the teams were split into two groups of seven, with the top four from each group advancing to a straight knockout phase.

FROM THE START OF THE COMPETITION all eyes were on India. The tournament co-hosts had become the world's No.1 Test team – but could they transform that form into the one-day arena? Their diehard fans did not just expect it; following their team's dismal showing in the Caribbean four years earlier, they demanded it.

India began their Group B campaign with a comfortable 87-run victory over co-hosts Bangladesh in Dhaka, tied a thriller against England in Bangalore, and then recorded comfortable five-wicket victories over Ireland and the Netherlands. They disappointed against South Africa in Nagpur, but did enough to qualify for the last eight. South Africa overcame a six-run defeat to England to qualify, as did England, despite suffering a shock three-wicket defeat to Ireland. The Windies were the group's final qualifier.

Pakistan and Sri Lanka were the form sides of Group A, with both winning five of their six matches to progress. Australia's *ICC* Cricket World Cup-winning streak (34 matches) came to an end when they lost to Pakistan in Colombo, but they did enough to qualify, as did New Zealand, who counted an impressive 110-run victory over Pakistan among their four group victories.

The tournament hotted up in the quarter-finals. Pakistan beat the Windies by 10 wickets in Dhaka; India edged past Australia in Ahmedabad; New Zealand proved too strong for South Africa in Dhaka; and Sri Lanka cantered to a 10-wicket victory over England in Colombo.

Both semi-finals were one-sided affairs. In the first, in Colombo, Sri Lanka dismissed New Zealand for 217 and reached the target for the loss of five wickets with 3.1 overs to spare. In the second, in Mohali, India posted 260 for 9 against their great rivals Pakistan, whose reply never got going and they, ultimately, fell 29 runs short.

And so to the final in Mumbai. Could Sri Lanka spoil the party? Mahela Jayawardene did his brilliant best, hitting an unbeaten 103 off 88 balls as Sri Lanka reached 274 for 6, but then India, led first by Gautam Gambhir (97) and then MS Dhoni (91 not out), held their nerve to reach the target with ten balls to spare. A nation duly erupted in celebration.

Above: *MS Dhoni (India) batting against Sri Lanka during the ICC Cricket World Cup 2011 final.*

2015

CHAMPIONS: AUSTRALIA
TEAMS: 14
HOSTS: AUSTRALIA AND
NEW ZEALAND

Australia and New Zealand co-hosted the biggest and, arguably, the best *ICC Cricket World Cup* to date in 2015. Notably, for the first time since 1987, the tournament's format was unaltered from the previous one.

NEW ZEALAND WERE THE SURPRISE package of Group A, winning all six of their matches, including a scintillating one-wicket victory over Australia in Auckland. Australia suffered no further losses to join them in the quarter-finals, as did Sri Lanka, who notched up four wins. The race for the final last-eight spot provided one of the tournament's biggest sub-plots. England would have been most people's pre-tournament picks, but they lost their opening two matches to New Zealand and Australia, beat Scotland and suffered a comprehensive defeat to Sri Lanka. It

Above: *Mitchell Johnson celebrates taking another wicket during Australia's victory at the MCG.*

Opposite: *Michael Clarke (Australia) batting against New Zealand during the ICC Cricket World Cup 2015 final.*

left them needing to win both of their final group games to progress, but they could not get past Bangladesh in Adelaide. Bangladesh batted first and posted 275 for 7; England slipped to 163 for 6 in reply before Jos Buttler slammed his way to 65, but England fell 15 runs short. Bangladesh's reward was a place in the quarter-finals.

There were few surprises in Group B. India won all six of their matches to top the group; South Africa and Pakistan both recorded four wins apiece to join them; while the Windies, who lost to Ireland but beat Pakistan, were the final qualifier.

In the quarter-finals, South Africa's spinners, Imran Tahir (4 for 26) and JP Duminy (3 for 29) ripped through Sri Lanka at the SCG, dismissing them for 133 to set up a nine-wicket victory. India crushed Bangladesh by 109 runs in Melbourne; Australia beat Pakistan by six wickets in Adelaide; while New Zealand beat the Windies by 143 runs in Wellington, with opener Martin Guptill smashing a tournament-record 237 not out.

In the first semi-final in Auckland, New Zealand ensured South Africa's *ICC Cricket World Cup* misery continued when they won by four wickets with one ball to spare. At Sydney, Australia's batsmen, led by Steve Smith (105), posted 328 for 7 and enjoyed a 95-run victory over India.

It was Australia's bowlers who won the day in the final, though. The two Mitchells, Johnson (3 for 30) and Starc (2 for 20) were the pick as they skittled New Zealand for an under-par 183. Australia, led by captain Michael Clarke's unbeaten 74, reached the target with 16.5 overs to spare.

7 MAGIC MOMENTS:

Hometown success for Sachin

The *ICC Cricket World Cup 2011* was staged in Bangladesh, India and Sri Lanka, with the final played at the Wankhede Stadium in Mumbai. This was going to be Sachin Tendulkar's last *ICC Cricket World Cup*: what better way for the game's biggest icon to bow out than to win the game's biggest prize in his hometown stadium? And it played out that way: India reached the final alongside Sri Lanka, who, led by Mahela Jayawardene's imperious unbeaten 103, posted a challenging total of 274 for 6. The stage was set for Sachin, but he was dismissed for 18. The stadium was hushed, before Gautam Gambhir (97) and MS Dhoni (91 not out) saved the day, leading India to victory with ten balls to spare. The dream had come true, and the sight of Sachin being carried around the stadium on his team-mates' shoulders is one of the *ICC Cricket World Cup's* most-enduring moments.

Opposite: Though he himself was dismissed for just 18, Sachin Tendulkar's fairy tale farewell was not to be denied.

ICC CRICKET WORLD CUP FACTS & STATS

From the greatest innings in the tournament's history and the most runs scored by any batsman, to the competition's best bowlers and most prolific fielders, the *ICC* Cricket World Cup has generated seen a number of scintillating performances and witnessed a host of records. The best of these can be seen in the following pages.

Opposite: *Indian legend Sachin Tendulkar holds a number of ICC Cricket World Cup records, including most total runs, most runs scored in a tournament, and most hundreds.*

ICC Cricket World Cup FACTS & STATS: TEAMS

Tournament winners

1975 Windies	**1992** Pakistan	**2007** Australia
1979 Windies	**1996** Sri Lanka	**2011** India
1983 India	**1999** Australia	**2015** Australia
1987 Australia	**2003** Australia	

Most tournament wins: by team

5 Australia	(1987, 1999, 2003, 2007, 2015)
2 India	(1983, 2011)
Windies	(1975, 1979)
1 Pakistan	(1992)
Sri Lanka	(1996)

ICC Cricket World Cup: all-time league table (by win percentage)

Pos	Team	(Span)	Mat	Won	Lost	Tied	NR	%
1	Australia	(1975–2015)	84	62	20	1	1	75.30
2	South Africa	(1992–2015)	55	35	18	2	0	65.45
3	India	(1975–2015)	75	46	27	1	1	62.83
4	New Zealand	(1975–2015)	79	48	30	0	1	61.53
5	Windies	(1975–2015)	71	41	29	0	1	58.57
6	England	(1975–2015)	72	41	29	1	1	58.45
7	Pakistan	(1975–2015)	71	40	29	0	2	57.97
8	Sri Lanka	(1975–2015)	73	35	35	1	2	50.00
9	Ireland	(2007–2015)	21	7	13	1	0	35.71
10	Bangladesh	(1999–2015)	32	11	20	0	1	35.48
11	Kenya	(1996–2011)	29	6	22	0	1	21.42
12	Zimbabwe	(1983–2015)	57	11	42	1	3	21.29
13	Afghanistan	(2015)	6	1	5	0	0	16.66
14	Canada	(1979–2011)	18	2	16	0	0	11.11
15	Netherlands	(1996–2011)	20	2	18	0	0	10.00
16	UAE	(1996–2015)	11	1	10	0	0	9.09
17	Bermuda	(2007)	3	0	3	0	0	0.00
=	East Africa	(1975)	3	0	3	0	0	0.00
=	Namibia	(2003)	6	0	6	0	0	0.00
=	Scotland	(1999–2015)	14	0	14	0	0	0.00

Highest totals: top five

Pos	Score	Team	Opponent	Ground	Date
1	417/6	Australia	Afghanistan	Perth	4 Mar 2015
2	413/5	India	Bermuda	Port of Spain	19 Mar 2007
3	411/4	South Africa	Ireland	Canberra	3 Mar 2015
4	408/5	South Africa	Windies	Sydney	27 Feb 2015
5	398/5	Sri Lanka	Kenya	Kandy	6 Mar 1996

Lowest totals: top five

Pos	Score	Team	Opponent	Ground	Date
1	36	Canada	Sri Lanka	Paarl	19 Feb 2003
2	45	Canada	England	Manchester	13 Jun 1979
=	45	Namibia	Australia	Potchefstroom	27 Feb 2003
4	58	Bangladesh	Windies	Dhaka	4 Mar 2011
5	68	Scotland	Windies	Leicester	27 May 1999

Biggest wins batting second:

By 10 wickets: There have been 11 10-wicket victories, two each for New Zealand, South Africa, Sri Lanka and Windies, and one each for Australia, India and Pakistan

Opposite: Australia's five ICC Cricket World Cup wins is more than twice as many as their nearest rivals.

Biggest margin of victory (by runs): top five

Pos	Margin	Winner	Target	Opposition	Ground	Match Date
1	275 runs	Australia	418	Afghanistan	Perth	4 Mar 2015
2	257 runs	India	414	Bermuda	Port of Spain	19 Mar 2007
=	257 runs	South Africa	409	Windies	Sydney	27 Feb 2015
4	256 runs	Australia	302	Namibia	Potchefstroom	27 Feb 2003
5	243 runs	Sri Lanka	322	Bermuda	Port of Spain	15 Mar 2007

Most balls remaining in winning run chase: top five

Pos	Balls Rem	Winner	Margin	Target	Overs/Max	Opposition	Ground	Match Date
1	277	England	8 wickets	46	13.5/60.0	Canada	Manchester	13 Jun 1979
2	272	Sri Lanka	9 wickets	37	4.4/50.0	Canada	Paarl	19 Feb 2003
3	252	New Zealand	10 wickets	70	8.0/50.0	Kenya	Chennai	20 Feb 2011
4	240	Sri Lanka	8 wickets	78	10.0/50.0	Ireland	St George's	18 Apr 2007
5	239	Windies	8 wickets	69	10.1/50.0	Scotland	Leicester	27 May 1999

Narrowest victories

By one run: on two occasions – Australia beat India by one run at Chennai on 9 October 1987; and Australia beat India by one run at Brisbane on 1 March 1992

Tied matches

Team 1	Team 2	Ground	Match Date
Australia	South Africa	Edgbaston, Birmingham	17 Jun 1999
South Africa	Sri Lanka	Kingsmead, Durban	3 Mar 2003
Ireland	Zimbabwe	Sabina Park, Kingston, Jamaica	15 Mar 2007
India	England	M.Chinnaswamy Stadium, Bengaluru	27 Feb 2011

ICC Cricket World Cup FACTS & STATS: BATSMEN

Most runs

Pos	Runs	Player	(Span)
1	2,278	Sachin Tendulkar	(India, 1992-2011)
2	1,743	Ricky Ponting	(Australia, 1996–2011)
3	1,532	Kumar Sangakkara	(Sri Lanka, 2003–15)
4	1,225	Brian Lara	(Windies, 1992–2007)
5	1,207	AB de Villiers	(South Africa, 2007–15)
6	1,165	Sanath Jayasuriya	(Sri Lanka, 1992–2007)
7	1,148	Jacques Kallis	(South Africa, 1996–2011)
8	1,112	Tillakaratne Dilshan	(Sri Lanka, 2007–15)
9	1,100	Mahela Jayawardene	(Sri Lanka, 1999–2015)
10	1,085	Adam Gilchrist	(Australia, 1999–2007)

Highest scores: top five

Pos	Runs	Player	(Team)	Opposition	Ground	Match Date
1	237*	Martin Guptill	(New Zealand)	Windies	Wellington	21 Mar 2015
2	215	Chris Gayle	(Windies)	Zimbabwe	Canberra	24 Feb 2015
3	188*	Gary Kirsten	(South Africa)	U.A.E.	Rawalpindi	16 Feb 1996
4	183	Sourav Ganguly	(India)	Sri Lanka	Taunton	26 May 1999
5	181	Viv Richards	(Windies)	Sri Lanka	Karachi	13 Oct 1987

Highest score: record progression

Score	Player (Team)	Opponent	Ground	Match date
171*	Glenn Turner (New Zealand)	East Africa	Birmingham	7 Jun 1975
175*	Kapil Dev (India)	Zimbabwe	Tunbridge Wells	18 Jun 1983
181	Viv Richards (Windies)	Sri Lanka	Karachi	13 Oct 1987
188*	Gary Kirsten (South Africa)	U.A.E.	Rawalpindi	16 Feb 1996
215	Chris Gayle (Windies)	Zimbabwe	Canberra	24 Feb 2015
237*	Martin Guptill (New Zealand)	Windies	Wellington	21 Mar 2015

Highest score in a losing cause

156 – Kyle Coetzer (Scotland) v Bangladesh at Nelson on 5 March 2015 – Scotland went on to lose the match by six wickets

Most hundreds

6 – Sachin Tendulkar (India) in 44 innings between 1992 and 2011

Most runs scored in a tournament: top five

Pos	Runs	Player	Tournament year
1	673	Sachin Tendulkar (India)	2003
2	659	Matthew Hayden (Australia)	2007
3	548	Mahela Jayawardene (Sri Lanka)	2007
4	547	Martin Guptill (New Zealand)	2015
5	541	Kumar Sangakkara (Sri Lanka)	2015

Leading run-scorers by tournament

Year	Runs	Player (Team)
1975	333	Glenn Turner (New Zealand)
1979	253	Gordon Greenidge (Windies)
1983	384	David Gower (England)
1987	471	Graham Gooch (England)
1992	456	Martin Crowe (New Zealand)
1996	523	Sachin Tendulkar (India)
1999	461	Rahul Dravid (India)
2003	673	Sachin Tendulkar (India)
2007	659	Matthew Hayden (Australia)
2011	500	Tillakaratne Dilshan (Sri Lanka)
2015	547	Martin Guptill (New Zealand)

Highest career average: top five

Pos	Ave	Player (Team, span)
1	124.00	Lance Klusener (South Africa, 1999–2003)
2	103.00	Andrew Symonds (Australia, 2003–07)
3	63.52	AB de Villiers (South Africa, 2007–15)
4	63.42	Michael Clarke (Australia, 2007–15)
5	63.31	Viv Richards (Windies, 1975–87)

Highest career strike-rate: top five

Pos	Strike-rate	Player (Team, span)
1	121.17	Lance Klusener (South Africa, 1999–2003)
2	120.84	Brendon McCullum (New Zealand, 2003–15)
3	120.20	David Warner (Australia, 2015)
4	117.29	AB de Villiers (South Africa, 2007–15)
5	115.14	Kapil Dev (India, 1979–92)

Right: *New Zealand's Martin Guptill hit an astonishing 237 not out against the Windies in 2015, obliterating the highest score record held by Chris Gayle.*

Opposite: *India's Sachin Tendulkar has scored in excess of 500 more runs than any other batsman in ICC Cricket World Cup history.*

Most sixes in an innings

16 – Chris Gayle
(Windies) v Zimbabwe at Canberra on 24 February 2016

ICC Cricket World Cup FACTS & STATS: BOWLERS

Most wickets

Pos	Wkts	Player (Team, Span)
1	71	**Glenn McGrath** (Australia, 1996–2007)
2	68	**Muttiah Muralitharan** (Sri Lanka, 1996–2011)
3	55	**Wasim Akram** (Pakistan, 1987–2003)
4	49	**Chaminda Vaas** (Sri Lanka, 1996–2007)
5	44	**Zaheer Khan** (India, 2003–11)
=	44	**Javagal Srinath** (India, 1992–2003)
7	43	**Lasith Malinga** (Sri Lanka, 2007–15)
8	38	**Allan Donald** (South Africa, 1992–2003)
9	36	**Jacob Oram** (New Zealand, 2003–11)
=	36	**Daniel Vettori** (New Zealand, 2003–15)

Best bowling in an innings: top five

Pos	Match figures	Player (team)	Opposition	Ground	Match Date
1	7 for 15	**Glenn McGrath** (Australia)	Namibia	Potchefstroom	27 Feb 2003
2	7 for 20	**Andy Bichel** (Australia)	England	Port Elizabeth	2 Mar 2003
3	7 for 33	**Tim Southee** (New Zealand)	England	Wellington	20 Feb 2015
4	7 for 51	**Winston Davis** (Windies)	Australia	Leeds	11 Jun 1983
5	6 for 14	**Gary Gilmour** (Australia)	England	Leeds	18 Jun 1975

Best bowling in an innings record progression

Pos	Match figures	Player (team)	Opposition	Ground	Match Date
1	6 for 14	**Gary Gilmour** (Australia)	England	Leeds	18 Jun 1975
2	7 for 51	**Winston Davis** (Windies)	Australia	Leeds	11 Jun 1983
3	7 for 15	**Glenn McGrath** (Australia)	Namibia	Potchefstroom	27 Feb 2003

Best bowling in a losing cause

6 for 23 – Shane Bond (New Zealand) against Australia at Port Elizabeth on 11 March 2003 – Australia won the match by 96 runs

Above: Aussie paceman Glenn McGrath has taken the most ICC Cricket World Cup wickets in history.

Opposite: Windies bowler Andy Roberts holds the record for best career economy rate, with an outstanding 3.24.

Most wickets in a tournament: top five

Pos	Wickets	Player (team)	Tournament
1	26	**Glenn McGrath** (Australia)	2007
2	23	**Chaminda Vaas** (Sri Lanka)	2003
=	23	**Muttiah Muralitharan** (Sri Lanka)	2007
=	23	**Shaun Tait** (Australia)	2007
5	22	**Mitchell Starc** (Australia)	2015
=	22	**Trent Boult** (New Zealand)	2015
=	22	**Brett Lee** (AUS)	2003

Best economy rate (min 10 overs):

0.50: Bishen Bedi, India v East Africa, Headingley (Leeds), 11 June 1975: 12 overs, 8 maidens, 6 runs, 1 wicket

Leading wicket-takers by tournament

Year	Wickets	Player (Team)
1975	11	**Gary Gilmour** (Australia)
1979	10	**Mike Hendrick** (England)
1983	18	**Roger Binny** (India)
1987	18	**Craig McDermott** (Australia)
1992	18	**Wasim Akram** (Pakistan)
1996	15	**Anil Kumble** (India)
1999	20	**Geoff Allott** (New Zealand)
		Shane Warne (Australia)
2003	23	**Chaminda Vaas** (Sri Lanka)
2007	26	**Glenn McGrath** (Australia)
2011	21	**Shahid Afridi** (Pakistan)
2015	22	**Trent Boult** (New Zealand)
		Mitchell Starc (Australia)

Best career economy rate

Pos	Economy rate	Player (Team, span)
1	3.24	**Andy Roberts** (Windies, 1975–83)
2	3.43	**Ian Botham** (England, 1979–92)
3	3.52	**Gavin Larsen** (New Zealand, 1992–99)
4	3.57	**John Traicos** (Zimbabwe, 1983–92)
5	3.60	**Shaun Pollock** (South Africa, 1996–2007)

Most runs conceded in an innings

Off 12 overs: 105 – Martin Snedden (New Zealand) v England at The Oval on 9 June 1983
Off 10 overs: 104 – Jason Holder (Windies) v South Africa at Sydney on 27 February 2015

Best career bowling average: top five

Pos	Ave	Player (Team, span)
1	18.19	**Glenn McGrath** (Australia, 1996–2007)
2	19.26	**Imran Khan** (Pakistan, 1975–92)
3	19.63	**Muttiah Muralitharan** (Sri Lanka, 1996–2011)
4	20.22	**Zaheer Khan** (India, 2003–11)
5	21.11	**Lasith Malinga** (Sri Lanka, 2007–15)

Highest career strike-rate: top five

Pos	Strike-rate	Player (Team, span)
1	23.8	**Lasith Malinga** (Sri Lanka, 2007–15)
2	27.1	**Zaheer Khan** (India, 2003–11)
3	27.5	**Glenn McGrath** (Australia, 1996–2007)
4	29.9	**Imran Khan** (Pakistan, 1975–92)
5	30.3	**Muttiah Muralitharan** (Sri Lanka, 1996–2011)
=	30.3	**Jacob Oram** (New Zealand, 2003–11)

ICC Cricket World Cup FACTS & STATS: MISCELLANEOUS

Highest partnership

372 – Chris Gayle and Marlon Samuels (Windies) for the second wicket against Zimbabwe at Canberra on 24 February 2015

Highest partnership: by wicket

Wkt	Runs	Partners	Team	Opposition	Ground	Match Date
1st	282	WU Tharanga, TM Dilshan	Sri Lanka	Zimbabwe	Pallekele	10 Mar 2011
2nd	372	CH Gayle, MN Samuels	Windies	Zimbabwe	Canberra	24 Feb 2015
3rd	237*	R Dravid, SR Tendulkar	India	Kenya	Bristol	23 May 1999
4th	204	MJ Clarke, BJ Hodge	Australia	Netherlands	Basseterre	18 Mar 2007
5th	256*	DA Miller, JP Duminy	South Africa	Zimbabwe	Hamilton	15 Feb 2015
6th	162	KJ O'Brien, AR Cusack	Ireland	England	Bengaluru	2 Mar 2011
7th	107	Shaiman Anwar, Amjad Javed	U.A.E.	Ireland	Brisbane	25 Feb 2015
	107	Amjad Javed, Nasir Aziz	U.A.E.	Windies	Napier	15 Mar 2015
8th	117	DL Houghton, IP Butchart	Zimbabwe	New Zealand	Hyderabad	10 Oct 1987
9th	126*	N Kapil Dev, SMH Kirmani	India	Zimbabwe	Tunbridge Wells	18 Jun 1983
10th	71	AME Roberts, J Garner	Windies	India	Manchester	9 Jun 1983

Most catches: top five

Pos	Catches	Player (Team, span)
1	28	Ricky Ponting (Australia, 1996–2011)
2	18	Sanath Jayasuriya (Sri Lanka, 1992–2007)
3	16	Inzamam-ul-Haq (Pakistan, 1992–2007)
=	16	Brian Lara (Windies, 1992–2007)
=	16	Mahela Jayawardene (Sri Lanka, 1999–2015)

Above: *Chris Gayle and Marlon Samuels formed the most formidable partnership in ICC Cricket World Cup history against Zimbabwe in 2015.*

Opposite: *No cricketer can claim more than the 46 ICC Cricket World Cup matches played by Australian batsman Ricky Ponting.*

Most catches in a match

4 – **Mohammad Kaif** (India) v Sri Lanka at Johannesburg on 10 March 2003;
Soumya Sarkar (Bangladesh) v Scotland at Nelson on 5 March 2015;
Umar Akmal (Pakistan) v Ireland at Adelaide on 15 March 2015

Most dismissals (wicketkeeper): top five

Pos	Dismissals	Player (Team, span)	Catches	Stumpings
1	54	**Kumar Sangakkara** (Sri Lanka, 2003–15)	41	13
2	52	**Adam Gilchrist** (Australia, 1999–2007)	45	7
3	32	**MS Dhoni** (India, 2007–15)	27	5
=	32	**Brendon McCullum** (New Zealand, 2003–15)	30	2
5	31	**Mark Boucher** (South Africa, 1999–2007)	31	0

Most dismissals in an innings

6 – Adam Gilchrist (Australia), six catches v Namibia at Potchefstroom on 27 February 2003; and **Sarfraz Ahmed** (Pakistan), six catches v South Africa at Auckland on 7 March 2015

Most matches played

6 – Ricky Ponting (Australia) between 996 and 2011

8 MAGIC MOMENTS:
Guptill's fireworks

There was a time when a one-day century was big news, and when Windies great Viv Richards smashed 181 against Sri Lanka at Karachi during the 1987 tournament, many thought that this record would stand the test of time. But cricket has changed and by the 2015 tournament it was generally acknowledged that it was only a matter of time before we saw the *ICC* Cricket World Cup's first double-century. The Windies' Chris Gayle duly obliged when he scored 215 against Zimbabwe at Canberra – but his record lasted a mere 25 days. On 21 March 2015, in New Zealand's *ICC* Cricket World Cup quarter-final against Gayle's Windies at Wellington, opener Martin Guptill, having been dropped in the first over, smashed
a blistering 237 not out off 163 balls to post the highest score ever in an *ICC* Cricket World Cup match – and this record may take some beating.

Opposite: After surviving an early drop, Martin Guptill's historic innings featured an outrageous total of 24 fours and 11 sixes.

TOURNAMENT CHART

Group Matches

Date	(Time)	Team 1		Team 2	Ground, Town/City
30 May 2019	(10:30)	England	:	South Africa	The Oval, London
31 May 2019	(10:30)	Pakistan	:	West Indies	Trent Bridge, Nottingham
1 June 2019	(10:30)	New Zealand	:	Sri Lanka	Cardiff Wales Stadium, Cardiff
1 June 2019	(13:30)	Australia	:	Afghanistan	Bristol County Ground, Bristol
2 June 2019	(10:30)	Bangladesh	:	South Africa	The Oval, London
3 June 2019	(10:30)	England	:	Pakistan	Trent Bridge, Nottingham
4 June 2019	(10:30)	Afghanistan	:	Sri Lanka	Cardiff Wales Stadium, Cardiff
5 June 2019	(10:30)	India	:	South Africa	Hampshire Bowl, Southampton
5 June 2019	(13:30)	Bangladesh	:	New Zealand	The Oval, London
6 June 2019	(10:30)	Australia	:	West Indies	Trent Bridge, Nottingham
7 June 2019	(10:30)	Pakistan	:	Sri Lanka	Bristol County Ground, Bristol
8 June 2019	(10:30)	England	:	Bangladesh	Cardiff Wales Stadium, Cardiff
8 June 2019	(13:30)	Afghanistan	:	New Zealand	County Ground Taunton, Taunton
9 June 2019	(10:30)	Australia	:	India	The Oval, London
10 June 2019	(10:30)	South Africa	:	West Indies	Hampshire Bowl, Southampton
11 June 2019	(10:30)	Bangladesh	:	Sri Lanka	Bristol County Ground, Bristol
12 June 2019	(10:30)	Australia	:	Pakistan	County Ground Taunton, Taunton
13 June 2019	(10:30)	India	:	New Zealand	Trent Bridge, Nottingham
14 June 2019	(10:30)	England	:	West Indies	Hampshire Bowl, Southampton
15 June 2019	(10:30)	Australia	:	Sri Lanka	The Oval, London
15 June 2019	(13:30)	Afghanistan	:	South Africa	Cardiff Wales Stadium, Cardiff
16 June 2019	(10:30)	India	:	Pakistan	Old Trafford, Manchester
17 June 2019	(10:30)	Bangladesh	:	West Indies	County Ground Taunton, Taunton
18 June 2019	(10:30)	England	:	Afghanistan	Old Trafford, Manchester
19 June 2019	(10:30)	New Zealand	:	South Africa	Edgbaston, Birmingham
20 June 2019	(10:30)	Australia	:	Bangladesh	Trent Bridge, Nottingham
21 June 2019	(10:30)	England	:	Sri Lanka	Headingley, Leeds
22 June 2019	(10:30)	Afghanistan	:	India	Hampshire Bowl, Southampton
22 June 2019	(13:30)	New Zealand	:	West Indies	Old Trafford, Manchester
23 June 2019	(10:30)	Pakistan	:	South Africa	Lord's, London
24 June 2019	(10:30)	Afghanistan	:	Bangladesh	Hampshire Bowl, Southampton
25 June 2019	(10:30)	England	:	Australia	Lord's, London
26 June 2019	(10:30)	New Zealand	:	Pakistan	Edgbaston, Birmingham
27 June 2019	(10:30)	India	:	West Indies	Old Trafford, Manchester
28 June 2019	(10:30)	South Africa	:	Sri Lanka	The Riverside Durham, Chester-le-Stree
29 June 2019	(10:30)	Afghanistan	:	Pakistan	Headingley, Leeds

Most finals hosted:

4 – Lord's Cricket Ground, London:
1975, 1979, 1983, 1999

Date	Time	Team 1		Team 2	Ground
29 June 2019	(13:30)	Australia	:	New Zealand	Lord's, London
30 June 2019	(10:30)	England	:	India	Edgbaston, Birmingham
1 July 2019	(10:30)	Sri Lanka	:	West Indies	The Riverside Durham, Chester-le-Street
2 July 2019	(10:30)	Bangladesh	:	India	Edgbaston, Birmingham
3 July 2019	(10:30)	England	:	New Zealand	The Riverside Durham, Chester-le-Street
4 July 2019	(10:30)	Afghanistan	:	West Indies	Headingley, Leeds
5 July 2019	(10:30)	Bangladesh	:	Pakistan	Lord's, London
6 July 2019	(10:30)	India	:	Sri Lanka	Headingley, Leeds
6 July 2019	(13:30)	Australia	:	South Africa	Old Trafford, Manchester

KEY: Start times are BST; all 13:30 matches are day/night games

Final group-stage table

Pos	Team	Pld	W	L	T	NR	Pts	NRR	Qualification
1									Advance to semi-finals
2									Advance to semi-finals
3									Advance to semi-finals
4									Advance to semi-finals
5									Eliminated
6									Eliminated
7									Eliminated
8									Eliminated
9									Eliminated
10									Eliminated

Semi-finals

Date	(Time)	Team 1		Team 2	Ground
9 July 2019	(10:30)	Qualifier 1	:	Qualifier 4	Old Trafford, Manchester
11 July 2019	(10:30)	Qualifier 2	:	Qualifier 3	Edgbaston, Birmingham

Final

14 July 2019	(10:30)	Winner semi-final 1	:	Winner semi-final 2	Lord's, London

CREDITS

The publishers would like to thank the following sources for their kind permission to reproduce the pictures in this book. Key: T=top, B=bottom, L=left, R=right.

ALL PHOTOGRAPHY © GETTY IMAGES: /Allsport: 50, 54TL; /Anthony Au-Yeung: 80, 124-125; /Scott Barbour: 98-99; /George Beldam/Popperfoto: 16; /Daniel Berehulak: 114-115, 118; /Hamish Blair: 51BR, 96-97, 120; /Michael Bradley/AFP: 119; / Philip Brown: 38TL, 52TL, 84-85, 87, 92, 93, 95; / Steve Christo/Corbis: 43TL; /Gareth Copley: 32, 53, 89, 90; /Graham Crouch: 109; /Charlie Crowhurst: 12, 15, 61; /Patrick Eagar/Popperfoto: 23, 36, 37BL, 40TL, 44BL, 64TL, 68-69, 78TL, 100, 105, 106; /Paul Ellis/AFP: 63TL; /Tony Feder: 58-59; /Stu Forster: 56, 57TL, 65, 88, 107; /Kieran Galvin/NurPhoto: 63TR; /Martyn Hayhow/AFP: 54BR; /Julian Herbert: 26-27, 28, 30, 74BR, 81; / Mike Hewitt: 8-9, 51BL, 70BL, 78-79; /Hulton Archive: 44TL; /Rob Jeffries: 75; /Paul Kane: 77; /Ian Kington/AFP: 42; /Ross Kinnaird: 82-83; / Christopher Lee: 41, 94; /Matthew Lewis: 13, 39, 71, 123; /David Munden/Popperfoto: 17, 18, 40BR, 60TL, 104; /Adrian Murrell: 48-49, 121; /Francois Nel: 46BR; /John Parkin: 70TL; /Peter Parks/ AFP: 122; /Ryan Pierse: 4-5, 110; /Pal Pillai: 91; / Ben Radford: 60BR; /Quinn Rooney: 6-7, 43TR, 67, 86, 116; /Clive Rose: 10-11, 46BL, 64BR, 73; /Tom Shaw: 44-45; /Phil Sheldon/Popperfoto: 24-25, 78BL; /Prakash Singh/AFP: 108; /Michael Steele: 37BR, 38TR, 52TR, 55, 57TR, 112-113; /Bob Thomas: 102, 103; /Darrian Traynor: 111; /Harry Trump: 21, 62, 72TR; /Graham Turner/Keystone: 101; /Lee Warren/Gallo Images: 19; Simon West/Action Plus: 33, 66BL, 66BR; /William West/AFP: 34-35, 74TL, 76; /Greg Wood/AFP: 72TL

Every effort has been made to acknowledge correctly and contact the source and/or copyright holder of each picture and Carlton Books Limited apologises for any unintentional errors or omissions that will be corrected in future editions of this book.